MW01232355

Modoc Jack

n Cents.   [Number 25.

Champion Novels

MODOC JACK.

NEW YORK:
ROB'T M. DE WITT, Publisher,
No. 33 ROSE STREET.

" When I looked again, and lo ! the palefaces were following them—
a great multitude with flaming to.ches—driving the red men, with their
squaws and papposses " MODOC JACK. Page 72.

MODOC JACK:

OR, THE

LION OF THE LAVA BEDS.

———◆———

BY CAPT. SETH HARDINGE,

Author of "Catamount Cris" "The Blazed Path," &c., &c.

———◆———

NEW-YORK:

ROBERT M. DE WITT, PUBLISHER,
NO. 33 ROSE STREET,
(Between Duane and Frankfort Streets.)

DE WITT'S
Hand-Books for the People.

DE WITT'S PERFECT ORATOR. 200 pages, 12mo. Bound in boards, 50 cents; cloth, 75 cents.

WEBSTER'S RECITER; OR, ELOCUTION MADE EASY. 200 pages, 12mo. Bound in boards, 50 cents; cloth, 75 cents.

FORTUNE-TELLING BY CARDS. 200 pages, 12mo. Bound in boards, 50 cents; cloth, 75 cents.

NAPOLEON'S COMPLETE DREAM BOOK. 200 pages, 12mo. Bound in boards, 50 cents; cloth, 75 cents.

DE WITT'S COMPLETE AMERICAN FARRIER. 200 pages, 12mo. Bound in boards, 50 cents; cloth, 75 cents.

DE WITT'S CONNECTICUT COOK BOOK. 200 pages, 12mo. Bound in boards, 50 cents; cloth, 75 cents.

WEBSTER'S CHAIRMAN'S MANUAL AND SPEAKER'S GUIDE. 200 pages, 12mo. Bound in boards, 50 cents; cloth, 75 cents.

WEBSTER'S BUSINESS MAN. 200 pages, 12mo. Bound in boards, 50 cents; cloth, 75 cents.

WEBSTER'S PRACTICAL LETTER-WRITER. 200 pages, 12mo. Bound in boards, 50 cents; cloth, 75 cents.

SWEET'S READY RECKONER. 200 pages, 12mo. Bound in boards, 50 cents; cloth, 75 cents.

ELEMENTS OF DRAUGHTS. 200 pages, 12mo. Bound in boards, 50 cents; cloth, 75 cents.

CHESS PLAYER'S INSTRUCTOR. 200 pages, 12mo. Bound in boards, 50 cents; cloth, 75 cents.

WEBSTER'S READY-MADE LOVE LETTERS. 200 pages, 12mo. Bound in boards, 50 cents; cloth, 75 cents.

CHADWICK'S AMERICAN CRICKET MANUAL AND GAME OF LA CROSSE. 200 pages, 12mo. Bound in boards, 50 cents; cloth, 75 cents.

The above list of books are emphatically the very best of their class that have ever been published. The editing, printing, and binding are all of the highest style of excellence, while the price is so low as to place them within the reach of all.

PUBLISHED BY ROBERT M. DE WITT, NEW YORK.

☞ *Sent by mail, postage prepaid, to any part of the United States on receipt of Price.*

MODOC JACK.

CHAPTER I.

THE OLD RUINS.

THE California Indians have always been a peculiar class.

Savages are not all alike. For instance, what a vast difference there is between the natives of the Sandwich Isles and those of New Zealand!

Fifty years ago, there were small settlements, called cities, on the coast of California.

These cities might have contained from one hundred to five hundred inhabitants.

Walls were built around these little cities to protect the inhabitants from the Indians who sometimes descended from the mountains and killed all who came within reach.

The civilized inhabitants were Spaniards, although a sprinkling of Englishmen, American, Irish, and Scotch was among them; but these were, for the most part transient persons.

Santa Barbara was a little city about as large as an ordinary square in one of our Atlantic towns; though there were several tenements outside of the walls, the inmates of which were always well armed.

In the year 1824, the savages made an irruption from the mountains and killed a number of persons, among others a stout Englishman who had resided at Santa Barbara a number of years.

His fate was remarkable on account of the great number of Indians that he killed before the fatal arrow pieced his heart.

It was long after the occurrence of this event when a singular meeting took place upon a hill not more than a hundred yards from the sea shore, and a quarter of a mile from the walls of the little city.

On this hill, was the old ruin of what seemed to have been a castle in the olden time, although it hardly seemed to have deserved that name.

On ascending the long hill, and approaching the ruin, a sense of loneliness and desolation stole over the spirits of the pedestrian, which was not a little increased by the fact that the moles, or field-mice, came boldly out of their burrows as if to withstand the passer-by who had invaled "their ancient, solitary reign."

It was certainly an evidence that few persons had ever visited the ruin on the hill.

The ruin was entered by a wide door-way on the side opposite the sea-shore; and the explorer was a little surprised to discover that the rooms on the first floor were more entire than the tumble—down appearance of the walls had, at first, led him to suppose.

The rooms were spacious and very high, the floor was square flags large and smooth. But, that was all.

Not even a stone or a piece of paper, or any evidence that the place had once been inhabited remained.

In one corner was a heap of rubbish piled up by the winds, which had free access to the old edifice, and which had heaped up dust and leaves sufficient to afford a bed for any forlorn wretch who might have strayed to those lonely precincts.

At the moment when our scene opens, however, the place was not entirely desolate.

A faint foot-fall might have been heard by any one standing in the vestibule, and then an object appeared in the large entrance room which was not calculated to reassure a timid adventurer.

The apparition which presented itself was a tall and very slender Indian woman, who seemed to be past middle age; and, yet, on narrowly observing her countenance it would have a trace, a discrimination that sorrow had added several years to her life which time had never contersigned.

Her features were strong, intellect—her eyes were very bright and piercing, but deep-seated—soon spoke in every lineament of her countenance.

This singular combination in the expression of her countenance was calculated to produce a nameless terror somewhat similar to that which one feels when awaking, with a shiver, from a nightmare dream.

This lonely woman in that lonely place wore nothing but a tattered shawl which was thrown over her shoulders, one point hanging down in front as low as her knees.

She walked from an inner room into the larger apartment, like a stalking ghost, as if she felt herself cut off from all communion with her kind.

Still, she listened very attentively as if expecting to hear some other sound than the echo of her own footsteps.

After she paused and turned up one ear to catch the expectant sound, aud often she glanced towards the door-way with an air of anxiety unmixed with dread.

But, she did not attempt to approach the place of entrance.

At length, she paused. She stood like a statue in the very centre of the apartment, as motionless as if chiselled from stone.

Thus she stook a considerable time; but, after-long waiting, she gave a little start, and a slight flush came to her cheek.

She walked slowly towards the door, and her dark eyes seemed to emit sparks of fire as a short figure entered the apartment so bundled up with clothing that it was impossible to determine his age and race.

The woman pointed towards the inner apartment from which she had emerged when first introduced to our readers.

The new comer went as directed and the woman followed him.

The room in which these two individuals found themselves was about half as large as the one which they had left, and presented the same appearance of nakedness and desolation.

The new comer threw off the greater part of his clothing and drew a long breath, as if glad to be delivered from the incumbrance.

When they disrobed the long-expected one presented the appearance of an Indian boy some fourteen or fifteen years of age.

It was easy to trace on the features of this youth a striking resemblance to the female in whose presence he stood.

The piercing eyes, the lowering brow—everything but the expression of grief was there.

Still, there was upon the juvenile countenance a peculiar pensiveness, such has been said by the superstitious, to foreshadow a violent death. One observes that sad expression in the portraits of Charles I. who perished beneath the axe at Whitehall; while, notwithstanding all his great vicissitudes of fortune, there is no such expression on the features of Napoleon the Great.

But, it would not, at this time, have been able to catch the ominous shadow on the mobile features of our young Indian.

He looked up in his mother's face full of animation, hope, and confidence; but, not until she had first addressed him did he presume to speak.

"What tidings brings the son of the Bright Feather to her of the desolate soul?" demanded she, in the Indian tongue.

"I have seen him," answered the Indian boy, joyously.

Trembling in every joint, the Indian woman passionately exclaimed, "Seen him!".

Then, after a slight pause, "And he is not here—and—thou livest!"

The two last words were uttered with a depth of scorn, mingled with anguish, which no pen can describe.

"Mother! mother!" shrieked the stripling; "cast

me not from you thus. Surrounded by a host of
armed men, what could my puny arm achieve? But,
mother, the time *will* come when the Son of Bright
Feather will avenge his father's wrongs, when he will
drink the blood of the palefaces as the hunted deer laps
the waters of Nondagura when the sun looks down
from the top of the sky mountains."

"Swear it!" uttered the woman in a voice deep,
sepulchral, and dreadful in its calmness.

The Indian boy slowly and reverently sank upon one
knee, and with one hand raised to heaven, he exclaimed
in a tone not so deep and calm, but as earnest as that
in which his mother had spoken:

"May my name be a scorn and a reproach, the
scoff of the young damsels at the corn dance, a spell
for evil spirits, and may I die the death of a dog, if
I speak true words to the white man, it ever I keep
truce with the palefaces, if ever I lose an opportunity
to cleave their hearts and to wear their scalps at my
girdle."

Slowly and silently, the woman passed her hand
over the head of the kneeling boy, until feeling that he
was forgiven, he rose to his feet, and stood with bowed
head before his mother.

After eyeing her son a considerable time in silence,
the woman once more opened her lips.

"And none suspected you?" demanded she,

"No, the disguise was too complete."

"Then, we may remain here till an opportunity
comes to deliver the captive from the hands of the be-
trayer."

"I heard them talk, mother," said the lad.

"And what said they?"

"They said they were going to civilize him—to make him a Christian."

The Indian woman's tall, dark, and slender form moved, almost spasmodically, a few paces towards the outlet of the room, and a sound like suffocation proceeded from her chest.

But, instantly, becoming perfectly calm, she stood thoughtfully, with folded arms and bowed head a' la Nopoleon.

She then spoke in her ordinary tone, like any woman addressing her own child; of course in the Indian tongue:

"Mahalala," said she; "you are the son of Bright Feather—the successor of a great chief. You are old enough to begin to understand the world; to see through the guile of the palefaces, and to learn the policy of your own people.

"Mahalala, when the whites prate in your ears about their civilization, they use the word *Christian* as the Indian brave uses the hide of an animal, in which he envelopes himself, when he goes to attack or to spy upon his enemy."

"Under this robe of *Christianity*, they conceal their purpose—their steady undeviating purpose—to rob us of our lands and then deprive us of our lives."

Here the lad interrupted the speaker by pronouncing the word "Miquon!"

"Ah!" exclaimed the woman, with a start, as if suddenly aroused from slumber; "you have not forgotten. It is well to remember; but not *now*.

"*Miquon!* it is a vision of the distant past: it is a

tale brought to our ears from the strong men who dwell by the side of the great waters. That *Penn* was greater than the sword—than the long knives of the palefaces ; he came not with peace in one hand and the sword in the other. He trusted our fathers and they trusted him. He came not with two faces and a double tongue, one speaking threatening of vengeance and the other professing peace and good will."

"But my son—the son of Bright Feather—speak not his name in those evil times. He and those who were led over the wide waters by the Great Spirit—had nothing in common with the creatures whom we deal with in these evil days."

"The palefaces of to-day come to us with forked tongues like the serpent; they long for the time when the red men will be crowded into the great waters of the West, when the last Indian will have been swept from the earth, that they may steal our hunting-grounds, and tear open the graves of our fathers with their plough-shares."

The woman continued speaking in this strain for a considerable time, and ended by telling her son that they must contrive some way to release Bright Feather.

"We have come over the mountains—we have sailed the rivers—we have traveled hundreds of miles in search of your father ; and now that we have found where he is secreted, we will not leave the ground, alive, without him."

Mahalala then produced a fowl and some large brown beans, with which the mother and son broke their f..st.

The sun went down upon Santa Barbara, the old ruin was wrapt in gloom, and no one dreamed that in that dark pile standing up in the moonlight were concealed two individuals more dangerous to the lives and property of the citizens than a score of ordinary felons.

CHAPTER II.

DETECTION.

On the next morning, the young Mahalala bade adieu to his mother, whom he left to her lonely watchings, and set out once more upon his dangerous adventurers to the walled city.

He was so muffled up as to present to view only his eyes and the tip of his nose.

This gave him a ludicrous appearance in the eyes of some sailors who belonged to a ship that lay at anchor within the distance of a quarter of a mile from the shore. They mistook the young Indian boy for a little old man, and they began to push and haul him about, when they discovered the superabundance of clothing in which he was enveloped. After cracking a great many jokes at his expence, the sailors began stripping off his dress, and then they perceived that he was only a boy—and an Indian at that.

They regarded it as a suspicious circumstance that this young Indian boy should be disguised in that manner, especially as they had heard of the inroads upon the inhabitants which were occasionally made by the savages who dwelt among the mountains.

The sailors fell to questioning Mahalala.

They asked him his name—where he came from—
and what he was doing there.

The boy could generally make himself understood in
English, and Spanish, in so far as signifying his wants
was concerned, when he wanted bread, he could say
'bread," and when he wanted water, he could say
"water;" but to explain the object of his present
mission in Santa Barbara, was beyond the compass of
his limited knowledge of the English tongue.

Mahalala knew an Englishman or an American from
a Spaniard, and would have felt perfectly safe in revealing to these sailors the whole history of his father
and himself.

He believed that they would sympathize with him;
and, in his juvenile simplicity, he would have hoped
for their aid in delivering the Bright Feather from
bondage.

But, in answer to the questions of the seamen, as
they stood upon the plains before the city, he could
only point towards the walls and utter the word
"father," accompanied with gestures that implied
chains and captivity.

The sailors comprehended the word *father* without
difficulty, but they were wholly misled by his gestures.

"Aha! blast me!" cried a stout mariner, whose
foul-anchor buttons denoted an old man-o'war's-man of
the British navy; "I thought so. His father is in
the plot. This is a young decoy duck; the old uns
are playing Bob-in-the-box. They'll break water after
the night-watch is set, and come down from the hills
like a whole clan of Highlanders —"

"Bosh!" cried a slender young man; "this is nothing but a stray lad hunting after his father. Let

him keep with us, and we'll make inquiries for him directly we get to yon goose pen that they call a city."

This view of the case found few converts; the majority coincided with the first speaker, and saw the necessity of making a prisoner of the young Indian, who, being disguised, they held, must necessarily be a spy.

Mahalala had keenly watched the countenances of the several speakers, and had gleaned enough, from their words and looks, to discover that his liberty was in danger.

Therefore, while pretending to be perfectly ignorant of what was passing before him, he watched his opportunity, and when he imagined that the sailors were off their guard, he sprang away from them and ran, with his utmost speed, in the direction of the mountains.

He had secured a good start before the seamen perceived his intention.

They gave chase, but in such an irregular and devious manner—not being accustomed to land travel—that Mahalala made his escape with ease, while such natives as witnessed the chase from a distance, supposed it was only a lark among sailors, and paid no attention to it.

When the young Indian had got beyond the inhabited district, and found himself among the groves and dingles, he paused as if uncertain whether to continue his route or return to apprize his mother of what had taken place.

No doubt, the sailors would tell every one they met that an attack was meditated on the town by the Indians, and that a young scout had already been detected and had made his escape.

Mahalala knew that well. Yet he could not contemplate leaving his mother in the lurch.

He believed that by taking a circuitous course, he could reach the ruin or hill without being seen by any of the native Spaniards.

Accordingly, he struck off in such a direction as to carry him far on the land side of the little city.

He had gone about a mile, and was cheering himself with the thought of reaching his mother before dark, when two men, in the dress of Spaniards suddenly emerged from a clump of bushes, and encountered the young fugitive face to face.

Both these Spaniards were armed with guns and long knives.

Every Indian in that region was regarded as an enemy; and, the Spaniards at once levelled their pieces at Mahalala; but, observing his extreme youth, one of them lowered his piece and said to the other, "Pugh! nothing but a child."

"He will grow bigger if we let him live," replied the other, still showing a disposition to fire.

But, the first speaker shook his head, and insisted that the lad should not be hurt.

"At least, then," said the other; "we'll make a prisoner of him, so that the young heathen may be baptized and brought up a Christian."

His companion reluctantly consented to the compromise proposed; and, forthwith, the twain approached the Indian boy for the purpose of laying their hands upon him.

Their purpose was not so easily carried into effect as they had anticipated. The young lad suddenly drew

a dagger from the folds of his dress, and kept them
both at bay.

"Surrender, and you shall not be harmed," said one
of the Spaniards.

"I will save us the trouble of shooting you," added
the other, aiming his piece at the heart of Mahalala.

He had pretended that he was about to give himself
up; and, having thus thrown the Spaniards off their
guard, he plunged into a neighboring thicket.

One of the men discharged his piece at the fugitive,
and the ball grazed the fleshy part of his arm.

The lad continued his flight, but the two Spaniards,
being determined to apprehend him now that they knew
he was armed, raised the hue and cry, which was heard
by several Spaniards who were hovering around a
large pot in which pieces of meat were boiling.

The women who superintended the culinary department, insisted that the men should go out and see what
was the matter.

The latter would much rather have broken their fast,
and they delayed to go forth so long that Mahalala had
nearly reached the embowered old barrack before they
sallied into the open air.

The Indian had perceived too late that, in his blind
flight, he had approached a nest of his enemies.

Three men broke from the covert just in time for
Mahalala to run into their arms. His two pursuers
came up at about the same moment, and halloed to the
captors of the boy to hold fast to the prize.

Mahalala struggled and kicked in vain. The five
men were, altogether, too much for him, and he was

soon tied hand and foot by ropes made of bullocks' hides.

Mahalala was taken into the ranche ; and, at first sight, the women took a great fancy to him.

This saved him from harm, as one of the first two Spaniards was loud in his censures of the lad who had drawn a dagger on him, and who came near inflicting an ugly wound upon his wrist, when he undertook to seize him.

The question, therefore, came up, "what shall we do with the prisoner ?"

Some were for taking him to the city to be civilized and christianized. That is to say, bound with chains and made to bear burdens till they agreed to be christians.

Therefore, the conversion of these Indian captives was, generally, effected in a few months ; and, they remained converted till they got an opportunity to escape and fly to the mountains, where they joined their old associates and were prepared to lead marauding parties, inasmuch as they had become acquainted with the topography of the white settlement, and knew where to strike the foe better than those who had never been captured.

But, the women interposed so clamorously that the nobler sex were obliged to listen to them.

They declared it was a pity that so fine a lad should be transformed into a beast of burden, and insisted that he was too young to be made a Christain of.

"Perhaps you are willing to be at the charge of clothing and feeding him ?" demanded one of the Spaniards, angrily.

"No," returned the lady of the house; "that is unnecessary."

"Then, you will let him go back to the mountains and join the murderers who come upon us, every year, to take our property, and our lives."

"No," answered the woman; "but Senora Valmaseda wants a house servant, and we will send him there by Phillippa Gonzalo when he goes with his mules, next month."

"And the Senora will thank you for your pains!" cried the Spaniard, scornfully; and, so saying he drew a long knife from his leggings, and approached the young Indian with a sinister gesture.

"*Misericordia!; quartel porel amor de Dios!*" shrieked the women; throwing themselves between Mahalala and the uplifted knife.

Whether the Spaniard really intended to kill the lad or not will never be positively known; but it was evident that the latter thought his life in danger; for, he drew his dagger as quick as lightning, and stood on the defensive, with flashing eyes, and undaunted aspect.

The men seemed to be highly amused at this chivalric display under difficulties; and he was left unmolested several days.

But, every attempt that Mahalala made to escape and return to his mother was frustrated by the watchful Spaniard, until the proper time came for packing him off to San Jose where the Senora Talmadesa resided in grand style.

He was fallen upon while asleep and tied, hand and

foot; he awoke during the operation, but too late to free himself.

When he found that he could do nothing to extricate himself, the lad became moodily silent.

Phillippa was charged to convey him to San Jose, and deliver him up to the Senora.

During the whole journey, Mahalala spoke not a word, though Phillippa was well disposed towards the boy, and endeavored to engage him in conversation.

At length, appeared in sight the bright foliage which surrounded the mansion of the Senora Valmadesa : the orange trees, the lemons, the forest of flowers, and the graveled walks, and the long, shady avenues.

Phillippa drove through an arched passage into the centre court, for the four sides of the house enclosed an area about eighty feet square. Into this central yard or court, the carriage was driven, and the lady sent a servant to get the news from Phillippa.

When the Senora learned that a house servant had been brought to her, she commanded that Phillippa should bring him into her presence.

Accordingly, Phillippa led Mahalala into a high, splendid apartment adorned in princely style, and presented him to the lady.

She cried out, at once, that he was too young for her purpose ; and she also said she doubted her ability to make him serviceable, as he seemed ill-disposed to tarry with her.

But, the Senora added that she knew of an English lady living near the sea-shore who wanted a boy; and, perhaps, he would be better suited there.

Phillippa was mortified at this reception ; but, he

hid his chagrin as well as he was able, and rode over to
the house of the Lady Winterton, with his charge, having with him, two assistants, so fearful was he that the
Indian boy would make his escape in spite of all that
he could do.

Lady Winterton lived at her husband's pretty villa,
within sight of the surf that whitened the Californian
shores.

With her were two daughters, Penelope and Angela.
Penelope, the eldest, was 19 years of age, rather a-
bove the middling height, well formed, with jet black
eyes and hair, and a very clear and dark complexion.

Angela, seventeen years of age, was, on the contrary
very fair, with large, soft blue eyes and a profusion of
flaxen hair which hung in natural ringlets about her neck
and temples.

The young Indian boy was introduced to Mrs. Winterton and her two daughters by Phillippa.

The lady, in few words, said that she thought Mahalala would answer her purpose; while the two girls,
though they said nothing, showed by their looks, that
they thought him handsome.

Phillippa was at a stand; he did not want to dis-
parage his charge; and, yet, he felt that it was hardly
fair to leave the lady without warning her that the lad
would escape on the first opportunity.

Phillippa took a middle course, and simply suggest-
ed that some boys would run away, and that she had
better keep watch of Mahalala until he had become accustomed to his new mode of life.

"I don't think he will want to leave us," said the
lady; "our treatment of him will not be harsh, and the

services which he will have to perform are not onerous."

Phillippa made his best bow, and departed, heartily glad to get rid of the troublesome boy.

As soon as Phillippa had withdrawn, Lady Winterton called Mahalala to her side, and, pointing out her two girls to him, asked him which of the two he liked best.

Without the least hesitation, he nodded towards Angela, and answered "that one."

Angela was too amiable to triumph over her sister, but, Mahalala had made an enemy of Penelope forever.

The black eyes flashed, and, with a curl of her red lip, she said scornfully : " I congratulate Angela on her conquest."

The mother only smiled, when Penelope resumed: "Is this young savage to be an inmate of the drawing-room ?'

" He will not stay with us long, certainly, if you speak of him thus," replied the lady ; " as he shows a preference for Angela, I think of letting him wait upon her, for the present. You will see that none of the servants molest him. To judge by the expression of his countenance, he is not so much of a savage as you would have us to believe."

" Do you know who made you?" demanded she; " have you ever been instructed in the catechism of a Christian Church?"

Mahalala understood, by these questions, that the lady wanted to know whether he was a Christian or not, and he quickly replied:

" No Christian. Christian steal land, Christian steal

my father. Christian kill all the red men and steal all
their land."

Penelope glanced at her sister, as she murmured :
" you are likely to have a gay time with your portege.
I wish you much joy, Angela."

Angela prepared herself to fulfil her mother's wishes,
and, how she did it one can scarcely say, but she was
seen by the side of Mahalala, soon after instructing him
how to hold a skein of silk while she wound it off upon
a ball.

The intractable boy appeared to be beguiled from his
evil thoughts—beguiled from himself by some curious
witchery exercised over him by this young girl of seventeen, so that it would almost seem as if he had forgotten his oath never to be reconciled to the pale-faces.
We shall see.

No one could doubt, who saw Angela and Mahalala
together, that the latter was, for the moment, enchanted
by his young mistress.

Whether she was equally delighted by him or not,
it was no easy matter to decide. She might have been
only carrying out the wishes of her mother.

When night arrived, it became evident that, although
the young captive was treated with the utmost gentleness, the lady of the mansion did not intend to neglect
the necessary precautions against his escape. He was
put to bed in a room so high that it would have been
madness for him to attempt to escape from the window,
and the door was locked on the out-side. He was
not aware that a servant slept on the sill of his door,
so that the least attempt made at escape on the part
of the Indian boy would have been effectually prevented.

CHAPTER III.

THE FLIGHT.

Two weeks had passed in this monner; and, although no disposition to escape had been shown by Mahalala, yet the watchfulness of those who had him in charge was, in no degree, relaxed.

The young Indian had seemed to become more and more attached to Angela, while, towards her sister, he had shown anything else but a tractable disposition.

It will be remembered that when the young captive expressed his preference for Angela, her sister resented it highly.

Still Penelope was too well-bred to engage in a vulgar brawl with a boy of fourteen, and he a savage. But, she was none the less dangerous on that account. She took every opportunity, by hints and innendoes to discharge Mahalala; and, when it is borne in mind that "a continual dropping wears away a stone," it may be imagined not only that some effect was wrought upon the master and mistress of the mansion by these tactics, but, also, that a spirit of revenge against Miss Penelope Winterton was cherished in the fierce bosom of the young savage.

"Jack," said the young lady to him one day—for "Jack" was the name which she gave the poor house boy—"Jack, is n't it almost time that you were christened, and that you were taught your catechism?"

Now, Jack knew very well that this was a taunt, and that it was spoken on purpose to annoy him, for neither

Lady Winterton nor her husband wished to force their religion upon him : therefore, he answered carelessly : —" That's just as Miss Angela says. She has not said anything to me about it, yet."

Penelope bit her lips, and sailed away with the air of Juno. She felt that the Indian boy, with an air of the utmost simplicity, had told her to mind her own business ; for he had reminded Penelope that her mother had placed him at the orders of Angela, and that she had no right to meddle with him.

Still, if Penelope had complained to her parents, they would have seen nothing out of the way, in the reply, of the young Indian. They would rather have approved his entire devotion to Angela, as Lady Winterton had given him to understand that the younger daughter was his mistress, and that he must wait upon her exclusively.

From that time forward, the bitterness of Penelope towards Mahalala increased in geometrical progression.

This gave great distress to Angela, who really liked the boy, and who imagined that he was attached to her in turn ; but she was too gentle a nature to reprove her elder sister, who might almost be said, lorded it over, the whole family.

At length, after Mahalala had been at the mansion a little more than a year, Penelope saw a prospect of glutting her revenge both upon the Indian boy and his young mistress ; since she knew that any misfortune befalling Jack would grieve Angela.

Jack had accidentally shot and killed a splendid peacock in which the whole family took much pride and pleasure.

When her father came home, Penelope ran directly to him, and so represented the case as to make it appear, that the young Indian had purposely killed the peacock.

But, unfortunately for Winterton's purpose, Jack overheard all that passed between Penelope and her father, and while his heart was ready to burst with revenge against the young lady, he resolved that her father's threat should never be put in execution.

Accordingly, he crept out of the house immediately, and finding the horse upon which the angry gentleman had ridden standing, all saddled and bridled, at the door, he threw himself upon the back of the animal, and dashed away at full speed into the interior.

But, Jack did not fly unseen.

The groom was not far off; and, he, knowing that he should suffer for his neglect if Jack got safely off with the horse, raised the hue and cry and hastily getting upon the back of another horse set out, at full speed, in chase of the run–a–way.

As for Mr. Winterton, already exasperated against Jack for killing his favorite bird, he was furious when he discovered that the Indian had had the audacity to run away with his best saddle–horse.

Giving a hasty order that all the men about the place should mount and ride after the fugitive, he sprang upon a horse and joined in the pursuit.

But, Jack had got a pretty good start, and having reached a forest five miles distant from the mansion without having seen any of his pursuers, he dismounted, and leaving the horse to shift for himself, he entered the forest and continued his journey in the di—

rection of Santa Barbara, where he had left his mother.
Neither Winterton nor his men knew anything about
Jack's mother.

Had they known that he had left his mother in an
old ruin at Santa Barbara, they would have so shaped
their course as to cut him off, and he would have
fallen a prey to his enemies.

But, his pursuers, upon finding Mr. Winterton's
horse at the edge of the forest, concluded that Jack had
shaped his course for New Mexico, and they continued
on till they reached the mountains, when they turned
back, Winterton being well pleased with having recovered his nag.

When Winterton returned, with his servants to the
mansion, he found Angela greatly distressed on account
of her servant who, she feared, would be treated very
roughly when caught.

But Penelope was so angry when she discovered
that the men had all come back without the run-a-way,
that she could scarcely contain herself; and her language, even to her father, was so violent that he forbade
her to come into his presence till she had sent an
apology for her conduct.

In the mean time, the young Indian was threading
forests; crossing everglades, and fording swamps on
his way to the old ruin where he had left his mother.

He believed that the palefaces of that region had
forgotten all about him, and that he might now venture there with safety.

As he lessened the distance between Santa Barbara
and himself, he became more and more anxious.

He had reason to believe that his mother would

continue to linger about the precincts where her husband was confined as a prisoner; but, how great must
have been her anxiety about him!

Then, again, she had depended upon him to procure
food both for her and for himself. Could she venture
abroad during his absence without immediately attract-
ing attention? and, in that case might not she, also,
have been seized and held as a prisoner?

These reflections quickened his steps, and he scarcely
permitted himself to rest at night.

Finally, "Jack"—as he was called by the Wintertons—began to fall in with the pale-faces; that is to
say, he saw them, but he did not permit them to see
him; although, being dressed in civilized habiliments,
and knowing how to speak English pretty well, he might
have passed himself off as a civilized man.

But Jack had no penchant for a civilized life; and
now that he was once more abroad and at liberty on
nature's wide domain, he felt how much better it was
to be a freeman than a slave, even when the latter is
surrounded by luxury and is treated with every indulg-
ence.

It would be untrue to say that Jack never thought of
Angela. His young mistress often rose to the eyes of
his imagination, with her bonny blue eyes and waving
locks, her rounded and graceful form, elegantly yet
neatly arrayed in the most costly garments.

He thought of her gentle voice, of the earnest manner in which she had always advocated his cause against
her sister, and of the many little presents which he had
received from her fair hands, all of which he had been
obliged to leave behind him.

He also thought of Penelope and her father, and then he renewed his oath that he would never make peace with the white man, and that his hand should forever be against the pale-faces.

It was evening when he entered the suburbs of Santa Barbara, he found no difficulty in making his way to the hill overlooking the harbor upon which stood the old ruins.

His heart palpitated as he ascended the hill, what if he should meet his mother outside of the edifice? would she be frightened on perceiving a stranger so near her, especially when he was dressed in the hated garb of the pale-faces?

He reached the old doorway—the broad entrance to the ruin.

The moonbeams shone into the hall and fell bright and cool upon the stone floor.

"*Anna!*" said he in a low voice. There was no response.

"*Anna!*" cried he, louder. Still nothing but the hollow, sepulchral walls echoed to his voice.

"*Anna! buccahdam?*" (Mother, are you hungry) continued the lad, fearful that she was unable to answer him from exhaustion, from want of food.

He now feared to enter and explore the crumbling apartments of the old ruin.

He felt a presentment that he should discover something of a sinister nature.

At length, after repeatedly calling upon his mother and receiving no answer, he ventured slowly to go forward.

He made sure that the entrance hall was uninhabited; then, he entered another apartment, and called loudly upon his mother.

There was no response; and, at length, after having explored every part of the crumbling edifice, he was obliged to acknowledge that his mother was gone.

His first impulse was to start immediately for his old home among the mountains where his father and mother originally lived.

But, the thought arose that his mother would not have left Bright Feather in bondage. She was probably lingering about the neighborhood. She might, even then, have only gone out to procure food.

She might return before morning.

Therefore Jack lay down upon a bed of leaves in one corner, and soon sank into a deep sleep; as well he might, for his travels and anxiety of mind had been incessant for several days.

But, Jack woke long before dawn of day, waiting impatiently for the morning light.

As he moved restlessly about on his bed of leaves, his hand or his knee occassionly came in contact with something hard; and he imagined that when he accidentally struck it with his foot, it made a rattling sound.

His curiosity was not much awakened by it, at the time, though he thought of it afterwards.

When, at length, the daylight appeared Jack got up, and, as he did so, on casting down his eyes at the bed of leaves, he saw that the hard substance with which his limbs had come in contact during the darkness was a human skeleton.

"My mother's bones!" cried Jack, sinking upon his

knees and entirely covering his face with his hands.

For a moment, a hope arose in his mind that this fearful object might be the remains of some straggler who had sought a shelter in the old ruin for the night. But, upon inspection, he ascertained to a certainty that it was the skeleton of his mother.

He knew her by the old tattered shawl that she wore, and by other signs.

This discovery not only told him that he was now an orphan, but it also gave rise to the most painful surmises.

His mother might have died of grief at his absence, she might have died of starvation, being deterred from venturing abroad to seek for food by the certainty of detection.

It is unnecesary to say that Mahalala, alias Jack, was wholly overcome with grief.

He sat for hours gazing upon his mother's skeleton, the picture of despair.

On the third day, he started up to go and look for his father.

When he approached the group of captive Indians in the plaza, he found that he attracted no more attention than any young Spanish boy might have done.

But, he did not see his father among the prisoners.

He watched his opportunity, and made inquiries after Bright Feather, of one of the captives.

He was informed, in few words, that Bright Feather had made an attempt to escape, and had been shot down.

His father was dead.

It was enough. He turned his back upon Santa Barbara, and started for the wild, the sworn foe of the white man.

Jack was now in his sixteenth year, tall of his age; straight as an arrow, and supple as the antelope.

He could no longer think of returning to his home, never more to be cheered by the presence of his mother, and to which the lines of Campbell would so well apply.

> "Seek we thy once-loved home,
> The hand is gone that cropped its flowers,
> Unheard the clock repeats its hour,
> The hearth is cold within the bowers;
> Our voices and our silent tread
> Would sound like echoes from the dead."

Alone and desolated, Mahalala wandered eastward till he fell in with a roving band of western Apaches.

With them he cast in his lot for a time; and, it was not long before he had an opportunity to wreak his vengeance on the people who had deprived him of his father and mother.

Three hunters were found asleep on the side of a hill, when Jack and two other young Indians clove their skulls with their tomahawks and took their scalps.

When Jack fastened that scalp to his girdle, he looked toward the west, and smiled.

It was his first trophy; his mother, in the land of spirits would see that he had kept his oath.

Jack and his two confederates were arrested; but, as it was deemed impossible that a mere boy should have taken part in this slaughter, he was acquitted, while the other two were hanged.

Jack stole a horse while all the people were attending the execution, and set out, at full speed for the North.

That is the last we heard of Jack until he had attained the age of twenty-two years.

CHAPTER IV.

THE TRAVELERS VENGEANCE.

A COMPANY well bestead with all conveniences for a journey, with equipage, fine horses, and loaded sumpter mules, lay encamped on the eastern sides of the mountains, at no great distance from Lake Kern.

Tents were raised and fastened down in the most approved fashion; the animals were picketed by driving stakes into the ground and tying them with a long lariat which afforded them ample space to move about and crop the herbage.

All seemed to be in high spirits. The company consisted of eight or ten trappers dressed and equipped for hunting, all well armed; a gentleman, his wife, two daughters, and a young son not more than four years old.

Besides this, there were a number of servants in attendance.

Preparations were speedily made for the evening meal, though the sun was still three hours high.

"Red Brand," said the gentleman to a strapping hunter, whose face was embrowned with much service, and on whose brow was the cicatrice of a long wound

which must have laid bare the fontal bone; "Red
Brand, do you think, we shall reach the Pass by day
after to-morrow, and do you never meet with any in-
terruption in this region?"

"As for the pass, sir," returned Red Brand; "we can
skersely 'spect to come by it so 'arly as that, and as
for interruptions, the red rascals do n't gin'ally turn up
near this yere spot. Leastwise I never seed 'em heah.
But, ef they war so onprudent as to cross our trail,
we've force enough to put 'em through, like wot war
never known before in these pairts—augh!"

"I don't doubt your readiness to do all that man
can do," replied the gentleman; "but, you know I run
a great risk in crossing this wilderness with so many
pieces of valuable goods; and that the safety of my
family is to be taken into consideration."

"It's a leetle wonderful to me," answered the trap-
per, "that the young squire didn't 'gree to meet you
half way, on 'count that he's payin' 'tention to yer young-
est darter. Not that thar's the leastest danger o' anything happenin' to her, but when one is in love, ye knows,
they're kinder anxious 'bout the lovely object."

The gentleman smiled at the well-intended officious-
ness of the rugged hunter, and said.

"You may well say that, under ordinary circum-
stances, Arthur should have been here to escort Angela
to his rural home in the desert; but, I presume he has
been detained by some unforeseen event."

"And it is that which I so much dread, papa," said
Angela, who overheard the last part of their conversation:

"I'm sure that nothing but some affair of pressing
necessity would have prevented him from meeting us

on the other side of the mountains as he agreed to do."

"You don't know how many events are liable to prevent a journey, Angela," returned her father, "a brief illness, a slight accident—anything, in short, is liable to derange one's plans. Besides it is not too late; he may be here to-night."

"Still, it is ominous," said Lady Winterton—for the reader has doubtless discovered the name and character of one our travelers —"I don't by any means, feel that sense of security which this good man's language imports. I must even add, that, since we have been encamped here. I saw something moving among the underwood !"

"Now, Priscilla," said the gentleman, hastily; "do not give way to such idle apprehensions, and say things that are calculated to alarm the girls; for, you know that they require a good night's rest after the fatigue of travel."

"It may be a needless apprehension," answered the lady, looking at Penelope, who had shuddered at the mention of the bushes on the hill.

"Of course it is needless," resumed Mr. Winterton; "this guide of ours here is too well acquainted with the customs of the Indians to be taken at unawares, and he knows every foot of ground over which we have traveled."

We shall see whether the guide was prepared for the anomalous enterprise of our hero, who, evidently scorned the beaten track, and chose to make his own trail while accomplishing his pilgrimage on this lower earth.

A rich repast was soon spread on the green; and,

Mr. Winterton, after offering thanks as a good Church of England man, bade the company lay hold and replenish the outward man.

The trappers and servants did not require a second bidding, and the viands and liquors disappeared under their jackets with amazing facility.

But the women ate sparingly, and were evidently in a state of trepidation. A cloud appeared to be resting on their spirits, like the lowering of the heavens before a storm, and this reduced their appetites to the point of nibbling a little cheese-cake, and playing with preserves with the point of their spoons.

At length, word was given for establishing sentinels and retiring for the night.

Half a dozen trappers took the first watch, and were carefully posted on as many points of the compass, forming a circle with the sleepers in the centre.

On saying good night, Penelope fell upon her mother's neck, and declared that she should not sleep a wink all night.

The fair Angela contented herself with asking the protection of God, and then she fell into a profound slumber.

But the Lady Winterton was too anxious for the safety of her husband and children to close her eyes.

It was far into the night, when the sentinels had been changed for some time that Lady Winterton heard a challenge.

"Who goes there?" said a voice which she recognised as that of one of the trappers.

Without waiting to hear more, the lady immediately aroused her husband and all the rest of the men.

all sprang upon their feet; but, after listening a few moments and hearing nothing, they believed that it was a false alarm, and they lay down again.

"Really, Priscilla, said Winterton to his wife; "you have broken the sleep of all these men to little purpose."

"I think not," said she, still listening "the sentinel did not speak for nothing. I would advise you all to be on your guard.

Penelope, who was, at that moment, standing by her mother's side, suddenly, cried, "Look there!" and she pointed off into the gloom.

All turned their eyes in the direction indicated by the finger of Penelope, but they saw nothing.

"I think, ladies, that you had better try to get some sleep," said Mr. Winterton; "you suffer your imaginations to run away with you. Fancy does wander when left to run its course unrestrained, and you have been so long deprived of sleep that it is not strange you see visions where others see only darkness."

But the ladies were not disposed to sleep.

Even Angela was now up and listening, with her mother and sister.

Nothing was seen or heard for fifteen minutes, when suddenly an arrow whizzed through the air, and coming unheralded out of the darkness, passed through the brain of Mr. Winterton and he fell dead at the feet of his wife.

She, uttering a loud scream, fell senseless by the side of her husband.

Of course, every man was instantly upon his feet,

and, at the same time, the dreaded war-whoop of the
savages was heard.

The camp was immediately surrounded by yelling
savages, and arrows flew thick into the camp wounding
many.

But the trappers were busy with their rifles and the
shrieks of wounded Indians filled the air.

The battle became general, in the midst of which
were the two trembling girls Penelope and Angela—
the former crying and wringing her hands, while the
latter was bending over her prostrate mother, and en-
deavoring to restore her to consciousness.

Blood flowed in profusion, terrible blows were
struck as the combatants engaged hand to hand ; but
the savages were too numerous for the little band with
whom they had to do, and, in the course of twenty
minutes, all the white men were either struck down or
made prisoners.

As soon as the battle was over, a young man, who
seemed to be the leader of the assailants, came forward
and glaring into the face of Penelope, asked her if she
did not know him.

She recognised him too truly as Mahalala, or Jack
whom, when a boy, she had treated with so much
harshness.

Penelope shuddered at this fatal recognition, and fell
down in a swoon.

By this time, Mrs. Winterton had recovered consciousness, and her wail of distress over her dead husband was heart-rending.

But the captives had not much time given them to
indulge in unavailing grief. It was evident that Jack

was apprehensive of an attack from the whites and the rescue of his prisoners. — ... The latter were all ordered to march; and, they set out for the north, closely guarded. ...

Three years passed away; and nothing had been heard of Penelope, Angela or any of the survivors of that dreadful battle, with the exception of Joe Raines, one of the servants, who made his escape just as the fight ended, and carried the news to the seacoast. ...

At the end of that three years, a young lady made her appearance at San Fransisco, dressed so much like a squaw that she was generally mistaken for one. ...

On being questioned, she gave her name as Angela Winterton ...

There were several persons in San Francisco who recollected distinctly the attack on the Wintertons and their fellow travelers; but it had been the general belief that the survivors of the battle were all put to death by their captors. ...

Therefore, the story told by the young lady in Indian dress was not generally believed. She was pronounced an imposter and the doors of all respectable houses were closed against her, while she refused to enter the abodes of the vicious or the vulgar.

Finding that she had no shelter during the stormy season, the authorities sent her to prison as a vagrant. There, she remained some weeks, and gradually sank into a decline. ...

Finally, the girl was pronounced by the physician to be in a dying state. A clergyman then call to see her, and to him she told her story. ...

"According to the story told by this girl upon her death-bed, her lover Arthur D—— had set out according-ing to agreement to meet her and to escort her and her friends to his villa.

"But he was waylaid by the Indians, and murdered. The same horde of savages who had murdered Arthur, attacked Winterton's band.—After the battle, the prisoners were marched North a few miles when Jack expressed his determination to put them out of the way, as it was too much trouble to guard and feed them.

Accordingly, all were murdered except Penelope and Angela; but they had little cause to rejoice in this distinction, as Jack soon gave them to understand that Penelope was reserved for the torture, and that Angela was destined to be his wife, he having loved her from the first moment that they met.

Angela was immediately made the wife of Jack, sorely against her will; while, a stake was driven into the ground, and Penelope was chained to it.

The marriage and the torturing were performed on the same day, and, although the screams of Penelope, dying in terrible agonies, reached the ears of Angela, yet she declared that she would gladly have exchanged conditions with her perishing sister.

She lived with Jack nearly three years when she made her escape, and after many vicissitudes, and nar-rowly escaping starvation, she arrived, more dead than alive, at the port of San Francisco.

Such was the story of the dying girl.

It is much to be regretted that there was not, at that time, some person living at San Francisco, who had been personally acquainted with the Winterton family; as he would have been able to recognize Angela Winterton if this woe-begone girl, dying in a prison, was really that young lady.

It is too late to learn the truth now, as no one can tell who or what the girl was.

Most people who saw her, declared that she could not be the daughter of Winterton, because her appearance and manners were wanting in refinement, and that her speech was not that of an educated young lady; but, much allowance must be made for three years' residence among the Indians, the wife of an Indian, and treated during all that time, more as a slave than as a companion.

The writer inclines to the belief that, that poor girl who died in a San Francisco prison, was really, Angela Winterton.

———

CHAPTER V.

MODOC JACK AT WAR.

We have now learned the early career of Modoc Jack in so far as history can enlighten us on that subject; yet, there are, no doubt, many events, many broils, and battles, in which he was engaged of which no record has been preserved.

Jack acquired popularity with his tribe by his wisdom, his diplomatic management of affairs with the whites and by his rash bravery.

Such was his disposition among the Modocs, a tribe of savages residing on Lost River.

The chief was named Sconches; and although he had his grievances, his father having been shot and killed by the whites—in which respect he resembled Jack—yet he was not a man of the same unyielding temperament as the latter. He was willing to take some pains and to make some sacrifices for the sake of leading a quiet life.

Some actions on the part of one Ben Wright, raised a doubt in the minds of the Modocs of the benevolent intentions of the whites. Troubles, disputes, and hard thoughts between the Indians and the pale-faces became quite common. Reprisals were taken by both parties. The whites continued to flock in and to settle the country in the region of Lost River, near the boundary of Upper California and Oregon, until a disposition prevailed to send the Indians to a reservation, that they might be prevented from stealing from, or otherwise molesting the white settlers. The Indian commissioner, about the year 1864, made an effort to get the Modocs upon the Yinax reservation on Martin River, in Oregon, fifty miles north of Lost River.

This, at once, raised up two parties among the Modocs, Schonches, the chief, being in favor of going to the reservation, while Jack opposed it.

It was on this occasion that Jack made his memorable speech.

"Brothers," said he; "the time has come for the Modocs to speak aloud, and no longer to hide their faces like squaws. What do you expect from this offer of the paleface? Do they ask you to leave barren grounds where there is nothing to eat—no venison to procure, no fish to catch, and to go to excellent hunting-grounds where the woods are full of deer and the rivers are choked with fish ?

"No, brothers, they want the pleasant land for themselves, and the worthless land they offer to you.

"Brothers, the time is come for the Modocs to show these palefaces that they are not squaws, but men, we can fight as our fathers have done; we can carry scalps at our girdles as the ancient braves of our tribe were wont to do.

"Think not, that I amuse you with idle talk. Our prophet—our great medicineman has had a vision, in which he saw my mother rising from the grave, my father with his head streaming blood, pointing to the settlements of the palefaces, and calling for vengeance.

"Brothers, the Great Spirit is on the side of those who fight for their homes, their lands, their wives, and their pappooses. He will give us the victory."

Thus Jack went on exhorting the Modocs to resist the palefaces until he fired them with the utmost enthusiasm.

But, Jack was well seconded by the prophet or medicine—man, also by a number of half—breeds, and interested white men who stirred them up to fight with the palefaces, expecting to reap a plentiful harvest by fishing in troubled waters.

Finally, after a great deal of talk, Sconches consented to go to the reservation, and he set out with about thirty warriors, with their squaws and pappooses.

The rest of the tribe remained, intending to fight it

out with the whites to the last, and these chose Jack for chief.

Then it was that Jack drew upon himself the notice of the whites, and his fame began to be carried abroad. He has been a terror to the white settlers ever since.

Captain Jack is, at the present time, a stern, dignified man, with a good head, though like all Indians, his forehead is low.

His complexion is dark—the pure copper color—and his eyes are black, full and piercing. His hair is long, hanging down to his shoulders, and he is of course destitute of all beard. His mouth is large, and its shape indicates firmness, determination and a great deal of character. He was very glad to see visitors, but he did not show it by his manner. When he shook hands it was with an indifference that, to one unacquainted with the Indian character, would seem to be absolute rudeness.

Besides Jack were several other noted characters, who united with him in opposing the encroachments of the pale-faces. Among these were Scar-faced Charley, the next noted one of the tribe. He has a Jewish cast of countenance; his nose being long and acquiline, and his face thin and narrow. He has a terrible scar on his right cheek, which, but for his natural pleasant expression, would make his countenance rather repulsive. He is about thirty-five years old, and is regarded as the bravest Indian in the tribe. He was very polite to his guests, and did all he could to make them comfortable.

Shack Nasty Jim is a youngster of not over twenty or twenty-two. Hooker Jim had a bad face, and though quite young, looked as if he could be guilty of anything.

The doctor was decidedly the worst looking man in the whole tribe. His face was absolutely devilish—narrow, contracted, with a little eye that twinkled its wickedness, and a mouth full and sensual. It was a countenance that would make anybody shudder.

Black Jim was a tall, fine—looking fellow, but one that few persons would care to meet alone on a dark night.

When it was found that Jack was placed at the head of the Modocs, great efforts was made to prevail upon him and the rest of the tribe to remove to the reservation where Schonches had gone, but Jack and others only went to examine the place, and having discovered that game was scarce there, they expressed their preference for the plentiful supply of fish in Lost River; and so they went back to their old home.

But, the troubles still continued. The Borderers hated the Indians, and they made no secret of it, while, on the other hand, the Indians regarded the Borderers as interlopers on their own domain; and, there were a plenty of mischievous white men and half breeds among the Indians who did their best to keep up this state of feeling among them, and to incite them to make incursions to the territory of their white neighbors.

At length, in the fall of 1867, Mr. Lindsay Applegate induced Captain Jack and his band to accept the hospitality of Uncle Sam, and they consequantly moved up to Yinax reservation. They remained there during the months of September, October, November, December, and January, and then returned to their quarters on Lost River. The Modocs since that time lived in this locality. Last summer the tribe were

encamped ·on· Lost· River in ˈtwo bands, one on each ·
side ·of ·the ˈriver.: Another band of the same tribe
camped near ·Fairchild's and ·Dorris ranches. Messrs.
Fairchild and ·Dorris concluded treaties with the Indians
and were allowed· to feed· their ·cattle ·on Butte Creek
Flat.:· · ·

· The first treaty was ·made with Ike;·an Indian who
claimed, the right over that section of the country.· ˈA
second treaty· was ·made ·with ˈBig ·Jack; and finally a
third· with ·Captain Jack, Sconches ˈand others.ˉ A consideration ·was paid the Indians on each occasion. Last
fall ·Mr. ·Odincal, ·the present: Indian Commissioner,
annoyed by ·the perpetual complaints of Oregon settlers,
determined to remove the ·Modoc Indians to Yinax reservation.:ˈ A combined movement· was consequently
made on Thanksgiving ·Day; ·last ·November. There
was a ˉbrisk fight between the ·United States troops and
Captain Jack's band, ·in; which upward of ·fifty Indians
and ·several ·soldiers ·were ·filled, and ˈmany wounded.
In the·· meantime :the settlers had· nearly prevailed on
the Curly-headed Doctor's band to go to the ˈreservation
as ·they stated; that Captain ˈJack's .party had surrendered ;ˈ but ·hearing the· firing! on the other side of ˈthe
river, .they ˈrefused to ˈgo,ˈ and presently both sides
·began ˈfiring. ·ˈThe citizens ˈfinally· retreated, leaving
one of ·their party dead on· the· field; and· the ·Indians
state the whites killed ·a ·squaw and· two papposses in·
the ·fight.· This party then: broke loose over· the country and murdered ·some .twelve ·or thirteen·ˈwhite settlers, and then: going ˈround· the· northern end of ·Tule ·
or ˉRhett· Lake, ·joined! ·Captain Jack ·in· the· lava beds.
Captain Jack and his party had retreated there· imme-

diately after their fight with the soldiers, but kept on the California side of the river, and went into the lava beds from the southern side. They did not murder any citizens on their retreat, and, in fact, told a settler name Samuel Watson to go home, as they only wanted to fight with soldiers not settlers.

The Indians, at lasted, started back for the mountains but were, however, induced to return to their settlement at Fairchild's, and while the latter was arranging to get troops to protect them to the reservation, they all started off one night and joined Captain Jack in the lava beds, reinforcing his command. Captain Jack refused to go back to the reservation.

The principal Peace Commissioners were Mr. Meacham, Rev. Dr. Thomas, and Mr. Dyer. These men were in favor of a policy similar to that which William Penn and his friends adopted towards the Linni-Lenape, the Mingoes, and the Shawnees, at the time they settled Pennsylvania.

But, there was a mighty difference in the two cases.

When the great chiefs, Metamequan and Tanirnend met Penn and his associates under the big tree at Kensington, they looked upon a people who did not believe in war of any kind,—a people who had come among them unarmed, and who had the full power to make and conclude treaties independent of any other authority.

The Indians saw that they were dealing with men of peace and only peace. The Quakers trusted the Indians, and, the Indians trusted them. It was no uncommon thing for the Quakers to go away to meeting, and to leave their little children at home in the care of Indians.

This proved that when the natives could become perfectly convinced of the peaceful intentions of their white neighbors, they also were disposed to be peaceable.

In the present case, everything is different. Although Quakers go to the Indians; yet the latter well know that the real power is in the hands of others; and that the military are at hand to enforce what the peace commissioners request. They see the bayonet protruding from under the Quaker's drab coat tail; as one detects the sharp nails of the cat under the soft fur of her paws. The Indian knows that if the gentle patting of those paws don't produce results pleasing to the Government at Washington, the sharp nails will appear.

In addition to all this, the Indians with whom the Pennsylvania Quakers had to deal, had not been tampered with by self-interested scoundrels who wanted to make money out of their blood.

Hence the labors of the Peace Commissioners proved abortive, and Captain Jack persisted in remaining with his tribe, in the lava beds.

These lava beds present a strange appearance. If one could imagine a smooth, solid sheet of granite ten miles square and five hundred feet thick covering resistless mines of gunpowder scattered at irregular intervals under it—that these mines are exploded simultaneously, rending the whole field into rectangular masses from the size of a match-box to that of a church, heaping the masses high in some places and leaving deep chasms in others. Following the explosion, the whole thing is placed in one of Vulcan's crucibles and heated up to a point where the whole begins to fuse and run together, and then suffered to cool. The rough ness of the upper surface remains as the explosion left it, while all below is honey-combed by the crevices caused by the cooling of the melted rock.

From the top of one of these stone pyramids an Indian can shoot a man without even exposing a square inch of himself. He can, with due haste, load and shoot a common muzzle-loading rifle ten times before a man can scramble over the rocks and chasms between the slain and the slayer. If, at this terrible expense of life, a force dislodges him from his cove, he has only to drop into and follow.

The country along the line seperating California from Oregon, in which the lava beds are situated, has been the theatre of military operations against the Indians at different times during the past twenty years. It has been traversed by emigrants who settled in the neighborhood, and it is well and favorably known as a cattle range. With the exception of the irregular volcanic region, south of the lakes, the land has been surveyed and laid out in sections. Still very little accurate information can be had concerning the retreat where the Modocs have continued to defy the power of the government. It is known, however, to be cut up with fissures, yawning abysses, lakes, high mountains covered with snow and abounding with caves. The lava beds cover an area of 100 square miles. They appear to have been brought into existence by upheavals from below. The roughness of the upper surface remains, while all underneath is honey-combed by cracks and crevices. The largest cave is known as Ben Wright's Cave.

It contains fifteen acres of open space under ground,

in which there is a good spring and many openings through which a man can crawl, the main entrance being about the size of a common window. In this cave, Jack and his followers fortified themselves. The gulches and crevices range from a few feet to one hundred feet in width; and many of them are one hundred feet deep. The Indians can travel through all these lava beds by trails only known to themselves, and stand on bluffs over persons fifty yards beneath and where it would require a long journey to go to them. They can see men coming at a distance of five miles without being visible themselves. They also can permit their pursuers to come within a few feet of the bluff and shoot down and retire, if necessary, to other similar bluffs. If pressed too closely the Indians can follow some subterranean passage, with which they are fully acquainted, and gain another ambush from which it would cost ten lives to dislodge them.

In the lava beds, are a number of small plots abundantly supplied with bunch grass.

The troops are well posted so as to prevent the Indians escaping. Their only line of retreat would seem to be in a southerly direction into the Pitt River Mountains. The tribes in that quarter are of a warlike character and have given the government considerable trouble in times past. In 1858 and 1859 their ambushes were so effective and their manner of warfare so advantageous that at first very litte progress was made in reducing them to submission.

The Pitt River savages, when pressed closely, would take to their canoes and paddle to the islands in the lakes, where they could not be followed.

After much care and trouble several boats were built and transferred across the lava beds, and the Indians were cut off from these hiding places. One of the latest measures of precaution taken by General Canby was to place boats on Tule Lake.

The troops, in pursuing the Modocs, had to follow them on foot, and in passing through the gulches and crevices must expect to find the enemy on the high bluffs above them at every point, or making their way through concealed passages to secure retreat. The cannon and howitzers commanded all approaches to and from the cave.

The peculiar geological features of the lake country in California resemble the county Antrim, in Ireland, in which is located the celebrated Giants' Causeway.

The scientific interest of the latter is enhanced by the beauties of its terraced formations and its great richness and variety of coloring. Like the lava beds, the basalt is from three hundred to five hundred feet in thickness, and like them, too, the pillars, caves, wells, &c., in the Giants' Causeway, appear to be the result of some great convulsion of nature, an upheaval equal to the effect of the explosion of vast quantities of gunpowder placed underneath the surface. Miners have not, heretofore, explored the lava beds, but no doubt there will be a thorough examination of this volcanic tract, which will always remain identified with a piece of very black Indian perfidy.

In this delightful country Jack lived like an Italian

Once in this basin there is but one way out, and that is by the trail we entered.

There are other ways out, but they are by tunnels

leading to the many caves or sink holes in another part
of the lava bed, and which will be more fully described
further.

On the outside of this basin there is a succession of
ridges as high as that which enclose it, but these do not
extend all the way around.   To the west of the basin
is a flat, table-like surface of lava, extending from the
very summit of its rim, clear back for more than a
mile.

In this level place are the sink holes or caves formed
thousands of years ago, perhaps in the cooling of this
immense body of molten earth.

The openings of the holes are very small; indeed
one does not see them until he has almost fallen in.
But they widen as they go down.

One can pick his way to the bottom without difficulty.   Most of these caves are connected with each
other and with the larger basin by subterraneous passages, so that one can go for half a mile in the bed without coming to the surface at all.

This is of incalculable benefit in defending the stronghold, for one man can keep one hundred at bay almost
anywhere in it without fear of being smoked out or
having retreat cut off.

After supper—which, by the way, was shared with
a keen relish by about a dozen naked Indian babies
—Bogus Charley came and said he would conduct us
to Captain Jack.

So the whole party gathered up their blankets and
followed.

Charley led the way right up one side of the basin,
through a little trail not easy of ascent by unpracticed

feet, and across the level place about fifty yards, when we came suddenly to the mouth of a pit hole at least forty feet deep.

The hole inclined as it led downward, and at the bottom widened and formed a perfect cave, extending under the rock at least fifty feet.

At the mouth of the cave proper, but yet thirty or forty feet below the surface a piece of canvas was stretched.

This was Captain Jack's front door, and the cave behind it was his abiding place—the palace of the Modoc king.

Behind the canvas we could see a bright fire burning, and nearly the whole tribe encircled around it, ready for the talk, which they knew was to come.

The descent into the cave was somewhat perilous, but by a vigorous clinging to the rocks and careful stepping, we managed to reach the canvas. Then, throwing that back, we stood in the presence of Captain Jack. It was easily seen that he was sick.

His eyes were dull, cheeks emaciated, and he was so weak he could not stand, but remained reclining on a huge pile of bear skins, with his two wives by his side.

Mr. Steele went up to him and shook hands warmly, so he did the rest of the party.

Then passing completely around the circle, all shook hands with the entire tribe. This ceremony lasted several minutes, and, when finished, we were furnished seats in the circle, near Captain Jack.

The only wood in the lava bed is sage brush; but this was piled on the fire with an unsparing hand, and the flames shot upward, and illuminated the cave brilliantly.

Then each member of our party lighted his pipe, and, after taking a whiff or two, passed it around to the right, beginning with Captain Jack, who took a whiff and passed it on to the next, and so on.

In such a large circle, of course, one pipeful would not go round, and so when it got smoked out, they did not hesitate to bring it back to be refilled, and then send it on to complete its journey.

During this ceremony not a word was spoken, and so the correspondent had abundant time to take a good look at the savages. Captain Jack was the central figure, and attaracted the most attention."

The Warm Spring Indians are a band of friendly Indians brought from the Warm Springs reserve in Oregon and were entrusted with an important duty. They acted as scouts and also to intercept any movement of the Modocs to escape in a southerly direction.

These Indians are known as the confederated bands in Middle Oregon, and comprise seven of the Walla Wallas, Wacos, Teninoz and Deschutes tribes, numbering 626 men, women and children. The leader, Donald McKenzie, is, no doubt, a half-breed, and well acquainted with the mode of warfare Jack and his party adopted.

The Warm Springs reservation contains over a million acres, located in the central part of the State, and the tract of country is such that nobody wants it.

The tillable portion occupied by the Indians consists of five hundred acres, and though even this portion is not very good land many of the families, by reason of their industry, have succeeded measurably in their farming operations, and are considered self-sustaining.

CHAPTER VI

NO PEACE.

After what has been said, it will be perceived that Mahala, known as Captain Jack, remained true to the oath made to his mother in the old ruin at Saint Barbara.

However he might temporize, and however often he might hold a " talk" with the men of the long knife, he was steadily and inveterately hostile to the palefaces.

He might make—or pretend to make—treaties with the whites, but he would never abide by them.

We have seen that the trouble with the Modoc Indians commenced as far back as 1872.

At that time the Modocs were prowling around Lost River, on the banks of which romantic stream they had their camp. They were great cattle thieves, and annoyed the Oregonian settlers terribly, and occasionally a settler would settle a Modoc, or *vice versa.* There was always some shooting going on between the tribe and the whites.

The government finally came to the conclusion to put its Modoc children in the Klamath Reservation. The Modocs were informed of this action of their Great Father at Washington, but they positively refused to go. They wanted to stay where they were— they did not wish Lost River to become lost to them.

When the government was told of the Modoc stand it was decided to use force as long as moral suasion didn't work.

So on the 28th day of last November, Major Jackson, of company B, First cavalry, with thirty-five men, moved on their camp at Lost River.

The Indians had scented danger in the air and were on their guard and their muscle. Each hideous face was besmeared with pigments, and each brawny hand grasped a rifle. There were no bow and arrow Indians, decked in guady blankets and moccasins, and with eagles' feathers twisted in their scalp locks.

Our red brethren meant business, and nothing shorter.

They were a band of seventy-five ugly looking wretches, with old shoes and overcoats on, and armed with Springfield rifles, revolvers and bowie knives. They were the Indians of the period.

A lively fight took place at Lost River, which resulted in a victory for the United States over the Modoc nation.

Captain Jack lost fifteen braves, and Uncle Sam lost one soldier. After the fighting Jack, his band, squaws and pappooses retreated to the Lava beds.

After this defeat of the Modocs, Captain Jack delivered a stirring address to his followers which, for its effect upon his auditors, might be compared to Robert Bruce's address to his army just before the battle of Bannockburn.

All sorts of skirmishing was kept up from that time until January seventeenth of the present year.

The government of the United States, satisfied that

it was at war with a nation maintaining an army of sixty unwashed Indians, was very cautious in its advances.

Three hundred blue coats moved upon the Modocs; a desperate struggle took place, which resulted in a victory for his highness Captain Jack.

Our forces retired in bad order, and Captain Jack and his dusky crew took to their beds again.

Attempts were made, from time to time, to come to a peaceful understanding with the Modocs.

The First Commission, composed of Mr. A. B. Meacham, Jesse Applegate, Samuel Chase and Oliver Applegate, Indian Agent at Yianax, as clerk, met at Fairchild's ranche about the middle of February, last. Mr. Steele and Mr. Fairchild, both old settlers, were engaged to assist them in their negotiations with Captain Jack.

After much unsatisfactory discussion in council the following terms were offered to the Modocs through Mr. Steele :—

First—To surrender to General Canby and receive full amnesty for the past.

Second—To be removed to Angel Island, where they are to be fed with soldiers' allowance and clothed until a new home can be provided for them and they are able to support themselves in it.

Third—To be furnished by General Canby with transportation for their women and children to the island, and thence to their new home, perhaps in Arizona.

Fourth—General Canby is of the opinion that he can promise that Jack and some of his head men should go to visit the President, and that the President will permit them to select for themselves a new home in a warmer climate.

They had a long talk over the matter; but from the first evinced a marked dislike to leaving the home of their forefathers, and finally sent back word by Mr. Steele that they would only live in their own country.

General Canby was opposed to granting the claims of the Modocs, and gave the following reasons:

First—They cannot live there without stealing, as their country produces nothing for their support.

Second—If the government intends to feed them it will cost 200 per cent more in the Lava beds than on any other reservation of a more appropriate nature.

Third—The country will be perpetually disturbed by quarrels between the Oregon settlers and the Indians; and

Fourth—Such acquiescence to all their wishes, after the United States troops had received a whipping, would be an encouragement to the Snakes and Pitnes, already disaffected, to make war and demand their own terms.

The second Commission composed of Meacham, Judge Roseborough, Mr. Thomas, and Mr. Dyar, was as unsuccessful as the previous one. Several interviews were held with the Indians, and Mr. Meacham sent a dispatch to Washington in which he stated the principal impediment to peace negotiations was the fear that the Indians indicted by the Jackson County Grand Jury would be given up for punishment. Meacham adds:—

"The Peace Commissioners and military are working together harmoniously said to overcome the distrust of the Modocs. But difficulty is encountered from the intervention of bad white men, who, from mercenary motives, desire a prolongation of the war.

"The desire of the government is well understood by my colleagues and the military, and no means will be left untried to secure peace."

There were at this time about six hundred United States troops in the neighborhood, stationed in different detachments. General Canby, commander of the district of the Pacific, and the United States Peace Commissioners, used every means in their power to arrange peace with the Modocs.

In their efforts in this direction they were not aided by the Governor of Oregon, who strongly protested against a peace. The Governor was in favor of a war of extermination against the savages. Captain Jack continued to make things lively. He, among other audacious acts, burned a log hut in view of the troops. A message was sent to the Indians stating that the President of the United States, General Grant, had heard about the war and was very sorry his children were fighting.

He looked upon all the people, of every color, as his children, and did not want them to spill each other's blood.

He thought this might have been a misunderstanding between the whites and the Indians, and he wanted to see about it.

That he was trying to have a new kind of law made, that would do away with war, and that's why he said "stop until we talk awhile."

The Modocs refused all offers of peace, and the Commission proved a total failure. A. B. Meacham, of the Commission, telegraphed these facts to Columbus Delano, Secretary of the Interior, at Washington.

On the 20th of March it was decided to surround the Indian camp, and reinforcements were ordered to the lava beds.

In the meantime it was reported that the Modocs were quarrelling among themselves, and that they had laid a plot to assassinate Captain Jack. Renewed efforts were made, time and again, to bring about a peace, as the United States authorities were opposed to bloodshed.

About the 1st of April there was a conference with the Modocs, which lasted several hours; and, at the request of Captain Jack, only Judge Roseborough, Mr. Meacham and Mr. John Fairchild were present.

There were ten or twelve of the leading Modocs with Captain Jack.

Judge Roseborough commenced the talk by explaining to the Indians the position they were in, and how he had come from Yreka to try and make peace.

Captain Jack and John Shonchin in reply reiterated their determination to remain where they were. They gave up the claim to Lost River, and said they would be satisfied to remain in the lava beds.

The U. S. cavalry then commenced reconnoitering with a view to active aggressive movements. The Indians said they would have "no more talk," Captain Jack was very furious and defiant.

The Indians built rock fortifications and otherwise prepared themselves for a desperate resistance. The

U. S. troops were held in readiness to move on the lava beds in force.

CHAPTER VII.

PREPARING FOR BATTLE.

It will be now seen that Modoc Jack was bent upon carrying out his principle.

Although he might have a talk with the whites, and might agree to certain terms, in so far as words were concerned, yet when it came to the point, he was found lacking.

His mother's bones were still white before his eyes; and, in addition to this fatal reminiscence, was the fact that three Indian chiefs who entered the camp of two white men to procure food, had been ruthlessly shot dead without any provocation whatever.

Mr. William Welsh, a gentleman who for years had taken an active interest in the Indians, and who was the originator of the Board of Indian Commissioners, said that he believed Captain Jack to be as honorable a man as could be found anywhere, and that if he sometimes acted in a hostile manner, he only imitated the conduct of the white western men.

Mr. Welsh also stated that he did not look upon the Modocs as being " a dirty, miserable set," but that he thought them very respectable and honest people until they came in contact with the whites, when they degenerated. The people on the border are their bitter enemies, and Mr. Welsh wondered that the Indians were not worse than they were.

We now approached the period when General Canby, Mr. Meacham and Dr. Thomas paid a visit to the Indian Chiefs, and we will preface the account of this fatal interview with a brief sketch of those gentlemen :—

General Edward Richard Spigg Canby of the United States Army was born in Kentucky in the year 1819.

He graduated at West Point in 1839 and served in the Florida war from that year to 1842, and was made Assistant Adjutant General with the rank of captain March 3, 1847, and was distinguished at Cerro Gordo.

He was appointed brigadier general U. S. Army July 28, 1866. During the reconstruction campaign he commanded successively the Fifth and First Military districts, and was finally, in command of the department of Columbia, with headquarters at Portland, Oregon.

Mr. Meacham is a prominent citizen in Oregon, and an intimate personal and political friend of Attorney General Williams, at whose suggestion he was appointed one of the Peace Commissioners to visit the Modocs and see if some arrangement could not be made by which a war with this band could be averted. He was for several years and until recently Superintendent of Indian affairs for Oregon. It appears that the appointment, though made with the best intentions, was an unfortunate one; as the Indians were particularly incensed against him, looking upon him as the originator and cause of their removal from their old homes to the reservation from which they fled.

Rev. Eleazar Thomas, D. D. of the California Conference, was the Presiding Elder of the Methodist Church in the Petaluma Circuit, State of California. The fervent piety, the unswerving fidelity, the zealous ministrations, and the Christian gentleness of Dr. Thomas, all manifested through long and varied services to the church, have graven his name deeply upon the heart and history of American Methodism.

The following was the situation of affairs in the latter part of March.

The prospect of peace with the Modoc Indians was not very promising, as they appeared to grow more independent every day, and consequently more grasping in their demands.

Mr. Meacham still represented the Peace Commission at Van Bremer's and was joined by the Rev. Mr. Thomas, a newly appointed member sent by the Indian bureau to practise the theory of moral suasion.

Mr. Dyer was expected from Oregon every day. Judge Roseborough would come as soon as he could leave his court at Shasta. Great things were expected from the new peace delegates. The Modocs were firmly imbued with the belief they could " lick" all the soldiers that could be brought against them, and consequently intended remaining where they are.

As General Canby was evidently getting rather tired of peace manipulations the troops would soon be moved into position surrounding the lava beds, and then some aggressive movement would be made in order to impress the Modocs with an idea of the number of soldiers that could be brought against them. It was expected that the mortars would have a very salutary

effect on their weak nerves, as in the last fight they expressed considerable curiosity about the guns that
".shot twice."

. On this occasion, however, only a few shots were fired from the howitzers, and none of them took effect,
only one shell bursting within the neigborhood and that
about one hundred feet above their heads.

A reconnoissance of the lava beds was made in force.
The object of the scout was to give General Canby
and Gillem a chance to examine the country with a
view to selecting a camp on Tula Lake, somewhere near
the foot of the bluff.

. General Canby and aid-de-camp, together with
Capt. Anderson, Major Mason and others left Van Bremer's at half past six A. M. and met General Gillem,
Colonel Perry and others at the bridge over Willow
creek.

The entire force, numbering over one hundred, rank
and file, then followed the trail to the top of the bluff
overlooking the lava beds and, were then dismounted.
They arrived at this post about noon, and Generals
Canby and Gillem got out their field glasses and took
a good look at the lava beds that lay directly beneath
them . The Indians were seen there moving about as
if in rather excited state, and gathering in about twelve
or fifteen horses that were scattered over the plains.

. Presently three or four of them took up a position
on a ledge ot rock, about a mile from the foot of the
bluffs; which appeared to be their first line of fortifications.

. General Canby now received a message from the
Indians, that Captain Jack and Schonchin would talk

with General Canby and Gillem at the juniper tree, half way between the foot of the bluffs and their present position.

The Indians occupied a fortification of about thirty feet front. It was originally a wall of rock about twenty feet high, with a projecting ledge about ten feet from the ground. On the edge of this ledge they had built a breastwork of loose rocks, about four feet high, which allowed them a space about three feet deep to work in, with the main rock at their backs. They were all armed, two with Springfield rifles, one with a Spencer carabine and the other with an old-fashioned Kentucky rifle.

Jack did not show any very great eagerness for an interview and thought Gen. Canby had better come where he was.

But, when two hostages were left behind, he seemed better satisfied and started to meet the Generals accompanied by Scar-Faced Charley, Steamboat Frank, the Curly-Headed Doctor, and three others.

The interview took place. Captain Jack was not very well satisfied with it; he said that he wanted peace.

On the way back General Canby said that he did not think Jack wanted peace unless he could get Lost River. Captain Jack told him as he was going away that if he had anything to give him he could send it down to the lava beds. General Canby asked him why they did not come out and meet the wagons according to their own proposal, and to that question he could not get an answer. The General was of the opinion that nothing could be done with the Modocs until they had experienced the power of the troops and thoroughly understood their position.

What was done after this interview of General Canby with Modoc Jack may be best understood by the following letter from the seat of war, under date of March 26, 1873:—

The Lost River troops marched last Sunday from their old camp and are now located on the east side of Tule Lake about three miles from Captain Jack's cave. The howitzers, under command of Lieutenant Charin, are with them. General Gillem and the two troops of cavalry at Dorris are expected at Van Bremer's to-morrow, and in a few days all the troops from the latter place will move into camp at Tule Lake, at the foot of the bluffs, about two and one-half miles this side of Captain Jack's cave. The Modocs will then be between the two camps. Major Mason is in command on the east side and Major Green will take charge on this side. If the Peace Commissioners do not succeed with "moral suasion," General Canby will probably try the power of the military. The attack will be made in skirmishing order, quietly, but firmly, and the troops will take their blankets and hold their position during the night. Under cover of night they will be supplied with rations and fresh water. The mortars will cover the advance of the troops and keep shelling Captain Jack's stronghold day and night. These tactics will, I am satisfied, have more effect upon Captain Jack and his band than all the "moral suasion" of the Peace Commission and Indian Bureau combined. I return to Van Bremer's tomorrow morning.

From all this, the conclusion is patent that the attempts at pacifying the Modocs were abortive.

They had their own private reasons for not being pacified.

They saw that if they did not consent to the proposals of the peace men, the military were at hand to compel them to do so, or send them on their long journey to the pleasant hunting-grounds beyond the Western sky.

They decided to exchange their present location only, for the pleasant hunting-grounds aforesaid.

Still, there was, all this time, a party, even among this handful of Indian warriors, that was disposed to abide by the decision of the Government, and reside on a reservation.

To these Jack observed that "to die by bullet not hurt much: to starve on reservation hurt a heap."

Therefore as the Modocs would not be ruled by the peace policy, General Canby saw no alternative but to try the war policy.

By some means, Jack discovered the real sentiments of General Camby, and laid his plans accordingly.

In the meantime the medicine-men of the tents were not idle. One of them stimulated Jack's revenge by relating a vision.

"The night was like the raven's plumage," said he, "darkness covered the earth, and thick darkness set upon the great waters, when I lay down by the foot of a mighty oak, and on its great roots I reclined my head in slumber.

"Then there came a sound like the rushing of a mighty wind, and a voice like the roar of the tempest, entered into my ears.

"My hair stood erect on my head, and my flesh crept on my bones.

"Then I heard a voice which was like the voice of a mighty chief when our fathers possessed the whole of this land; and the voice said: "Awake, son of Arroqueba!" and the voice said "Look to the North, to the South, to the East, and to the West!"

"I looked, and beheld thousands of red men flocking from the North, the East, and the South, and all of them travelling to the West—towards the setting sun.

"Some were on horses, and some were on foot. They had their squaws and their pappooses with them. The were all leaving the hunting-grounds of their fathers, and hastening towards the great waters of the West.

"Then I looked again, and the pale-faces were following them—a great multitude, with flaming torches —driving the red men, with their squaws and pappos-ses, before them, as if they had been nothing but a horde of wild beasts who had none of the rights of men, who had no right to their own lands and their own country; but who ought to be swept from the face of the earth, like so many wolves and catamounts.

"Then, there was a long silence, when the spirit said to me again *look!*"

"I looked again, and behold! the father of Mahalala stood before me, with chains upon his limbs, and his breast sending forth a stream of blood; and there suddenly started up from the earth a tall and slender form which took the shape and features of a woman; but with deep sadness on her brow, and sorrow had carved deep furrows in her cheek.

"She lifted her hand towards Heaven, and cried 'His oath! his oath! the oath of Mahalala!!"

"My mother!" cried Captain Jack, as he listened to these words of the "Doctor," delivered in tones of thrilling earnestness. "That was my mother!" continued Jack, "I will keep my oath."

"Then," continued the medicine-man; "the woman sank again into the earth, with a cry of veng ce that has rung in my ears ever since."

"Yes, vengeance," replied Captain Jack; "we will have vengeance, and nothing else but vengeance."

Such was the state of affairs, when the Modocs pretended they were going to remove to the reservation. A day was appointed and agreed to for the surrender to take place. Wagons were sent by the good-hearted Commissioners to convey Captain Jack's baggage over the rough ground; but no signs of the Indians were discoverable. Days passed, and at length an Indian appeared, who complained that Captain Jack and his fellows were fearful of the troops, and that they wanted to go to their old Lost River reservation. The troops under General Canby now moved forward again and commenced to encircle the savages in their fortress. The circle was drawn gradually closer, and the Indians again professed a desire for peace conferences. They saw the troops drawing closer, and closer, and now set up a new demand. They objected altogether to leaving the lava beds, and wanted the troops sent away. Notwithstanding this preposterous demand, the kind-hearted Peace Commissioners listened to the palaver of the braves. Several interviews took place.

The Commissioners, together with Gen. Canby, had

labored hopefully, and had apparently gained several points over the Indians, looking to a peaceful solution of this question.

For some time, all the Modoc schemes of treachery had been thwarted through the fidelity of the interpreter, Mrs. Riddle who was a Modoc woman.

Terms were agreed on for a meeting which were satisfactory to Dr. Thomas and Gen. Canby, but not to Mr. Meacham or Mr. Dyar, or to Mrs. Riddle, who expressed her apprehensions that mischief was breeding in the Modoc camp.

But Gen. Canby said that the Modocs dared not molest them as his forces commanded the situation, and Dr. Thomas declared that where God called him to go, he would go, trusting to his care.

On the afternoon of April 10th, 1873, five Indians and four squaws came into the camp and were made presents of clothing and provisions by the Peace Commissioners, and a message was sent out by the Commissioners asking for a talk next morning at a point about a mile from the picket line. Later in the evening Bogus Charley came in and told the picket that he could take his gun; that he (Charley) did not intend to go back any more. The picket brought him in and took him to the tent of General Canby where Charley left his gun and remained at the tent of Frank Riddle during the night. Next morning Boston Charley came in and told the Commission that Captain Jack and five other Indians would meet the Commission outside the lines. Boston Charley and Bogus Charley then mounted a horse and started for the lava beds. About an hour after their departure General Canby, started for the place appointed. The party arrived at the appointed place, and were closely watched by the signal officer, Lieutenant Adams, from the signal station on the hill over-looking the camp.

It was between ten and eleven o'clock in the morning when the Peace Commission party—comprising Gen. Canby, Mr. A. B. Meacham. Dr. Thomas, Mr. Dyar, Riddle, the interpreter, and squaw, and Bogus Charley and Boston Charley—went out to the designated spot.

There they met Captain Jack, John Schonchin, Black Jim, Shack Nasty Jim, Ellen's Man and Hawker Jim. They had no guns with them, but each carried a pistol at his belt. This, however, was not much noticed, as in previous interviews they had their guns with them.

They sat down in a kind of broken circle, and General Canby, Meacham, and Dr. Thomas sat together, faced by Captain Jack and Schonchin. Mr. Dyar stood by Jack, holding his horse, with Hawker Jim and Shack Nasty Jim to his left.

Meacham opened the talk, and gave a long history of what they wanted to do for them, after which Gen. Canby and Dr. Thomas both talked for some time. The Commissioners re-affirmed that the soldiers would never be withdrawn until the difficulty was settled, still extending the offer of amnesty, a suitable and satisfactory home, and ample provision for their welfare in the future. The reply from Jack and Schonchin—both chiefs—was : "Take away your soldiers, and we will talk about it."

Captain Jack then talked in an apparently good,

serious strain, and when he finished stepped back to the rear near where Meacham's horse was hitched.

Jack asked for Hot Creek and Cottonwood, the places occupied by Fairchild and Dorris, for a reservation.

Mr. Meacham told Jack that it was not possible to give him what he asked.

John Schonchin then began to talk. He told Mr. Meacham to say no more; that he had said enough on that subject, and while Schonchin was speaking, Capt. Jack was heard to say "All ready!" At the same time Mr. Dyar heard a cap miss fire, and, looking around, he saw Captain Jack to his left, with his pistol pointed at General Canby.

This was the signal for a general massacre, and a dozen pistols were fired inside of half a minute.

Mr. Dyar, after hearing the cap miss fire, turned and fled, followed closely by Hawker Jim, who fired two shots after him. Dyar, finding that Hawker Jim was gaining upon him, turned and drew his derringer whereupon Hawker Jim retreated and made the best of his way to the Modoc Camp.

Captain Jack fired again on General Canby who ran off to the left; but the ball of Jack's pistol struck him under the eye, and he fell dead to the ground.

Meacham was shot at by Schonchin wounded in the head. He tried to draw his derringer, when two Indians ran up and knocked him down-

Boston Charley and another Indian fired at Dr. Thomas. The first discharge brought him to his knees, and the second killed him.

Riddle ran off, and it appears they did not fire at

him, but they knocked his squaw, down. Dyar, Riddle, and the squaw returned in safety, to the camp.

About half an hour after the party of General Canby had reached the place of meeting with Jack and the other savages, a cry from the signal station was heard, saying that the Indians had attacked the Peace Commission, and that an engagment had commenced between the Indians and Col. Mason. In a moment the troops were under arms, and deployed as skirmishers, under the command of Col. Green, and orders were given to forward double-quick. Very shortly afterward Mr. Dyer returned and stated that the Indians had attacked them, and that he thought he was the only one who had escaped: but in a few moments after Riddle and his squaw were seen within the picket. Col. Miller and Major Throckmorton's two batteries, that were leading the skirmish line rushed out, and, after about five minutes tramp over the broken rocks, they arrived at the scene of the massacre.

In the distance were seen three of the perpetrators of the murders running round the edge of the lake on their way back to their rocky fastness.

About a hundred yards to the west of the place of meeting was found Mr. A. B. Meacham badly wounded with a pistol shot over the left eye. He was immediately attended to and carried back for medical treatment.

Fifty yards further on was the body of the Rev. Dr. Thomas, lying on his face and stripped to the waist. Life was extinct from pistol shot wounds in his head.

The body of General Canby, the hero of many a fight,

was stripped of every vestige of clothing and lay about
one hundred yards to the southward, with two pistol
shots in his head.

Pausing only to cast a glance on the body of the man
they both loved and respected, the troops dashed on
and the two leading batteries were within a mile of
the murderers when the bugle call sounded a "halt."
Lieutenant Egan and Major Wright's companies of the
Twelfth infantry were behind the artillery and then
come the cavalry.

General Gillem and Colonel Green and staff were up
with the men, but as soon as they found that the Indians had all got back to their stronghold the troops
were ordered to fall back with the intent of commenc-
ing active operations on the next day.

That the Indians intended a general massacre is suf-
ficiently evident.

The following additional account, given by Captain
Anderson, at the time, will not be found uninteresting:

Captain Anderson was at Colonel Mason's camp
when the attack was made on the Peace Commission
and party. He says Lieutenants Sherwood and Doyle
were allured out from the camp by a white flag. They
went 400 or 500 yards, where they met what they supposed to be only two Indians, who said they wanted
to talk to "Little Tyee" (Colonel Mason). They were
told that they (the officers) did not want to talk, and
for the Indians to go back to their camp and they would
return to theirs. As the officers turned around the Indians, four in number, fired upon them, wounding Lieutenant Sherwood in the arm and thigh, the latter being
a severe wound, the bone having been shattered by the

bullet. Captain Anderson, who was on duty at the
signal station on Hospital Rock, saw plainly, the attack
upon Colonel Mason's front, and telegraphed General
Gillem to notify the Peace Commission immediately.
Colonel Biddle, who was at General Gillem's headquarters when this message was received, at once placed his
field-glass upon General Canby as the party sat together
about one mile distant, and very soon afterwards he
perceived the whole party scattered. The Colonel followed the General's course with his glass while he ran
about fifty yards, when he threw up his arms and fell
backward dead. Two of the Indians who were following him jumped on him, and one—believed to be Captain Jack—stabbed him in the neck. His body was
afterwards completely stripped. Dr. Thomas was also
entirely stripped. His purse, containing about $60,
was found under the body, the Indians having dropped
it. Mr. Meacham was shot in three places, one ball
entering at the inner corner of his right eye, another
inside of his head, and the third passing through his
right forearm. The first two balls are both believed to
have lodged within his cranium. He also received a cut
in the left arm and a scalp wound about five inches long.
He was found about fifty yards from the spot where
the slaughter began, in a direction opposite that taken
by General Canby. He was also entirely stripped, and,
when found bewildered in mind. Captain Anderson
spent an hour with him yesterday morning, when he
was conscious and in no pain. Meacham says he thinks
he shot Schonchin in the abdomen, and blood was found
which indicated that one of the Indians had been wounded. The soldiers who were ready started on a double
quick immediately upon the firing of the shots. They

met Dyar and Riddle and his wife before they were half
way from the camp. The Indians retired, and kept up
their retreat about 600 yards in advance of the soldiers,
who followed them half a mile beyond the murder-
ground, where they remained until dark, when they
were withdrawn as they were not-provided with supplies.

CHAPTER VIII.

A BATTLE.

The news of this apparently causeless and unaccount-
able massacre rang through the country like a tocsin
calling for an immediate war of extermination.

Every letter from San Francisco containing the
slightest information in regard to the fate of General
Canby and his companions was eagerly read.

Among other accounts is the following sketch of the
atrocity, from A. B. Meacham, chairman of the Modoc
Peace Commission.

About this time two armed Indians suddenly appeared from the brush in our rear. An explanation
was asked, and Captain Jack replied by snapping a pistol at General Canby, saying in Indian, "All ready;"
after which General Canby was despatched by Captain
Jack with a pistol and knife, and Dr. Thomas by a pis-
tol-shot in the breast and gunshot in the head by Boston Charley. Meacham and Dyar attempted to escape
toward the camp, the former followed by Schonchin
John, and the latter by Black Jim and Hooker Jim.
Schonchin fired six shots at Meacham, hitting him four-

times and leaving him for dead. Schonchin attempting to scalp him was deterred by a Modoc woman. Dyar escaped unhurt although fired at three times by Black Jim, who was only a few feet away, and by Hooker Jim, by whom he was pursued. After running about 200 yards he turned upon his pursuer with a small pocket Derringer, when the Indian turned and ran back, thus letting Dyar get away. Mr. Dyar will be obliged to leave in a day or two on account of official duties, but while here the remainder of the Commission will consult with General Gillem should any active measures be necessary on our part. We believe that complete subjugation by the military is the only method by which to deal with these Indians. Very respectfully, your obedient servant,

A. B. MEACHAM,
Chairman Modoc Peace Commission.

The following was written immediatly after the massacre:

APRIL 12, 10 P. M.—The news of the horrible massacre of General Canby and Commissioner Thomas has cast a gloom over the entire community, and great excitement and intense feeling exist that the Modocs should now receive the punishment they richly deserve, and that not one should be left for this terrible massacre.

H. C. Ticknor, who brought the official dispatches, left headquarters at 5 P. M. yesterday. He said that orders had just been issued for an advance along the whole line at 5 A. M. to-day. The plan was to advance slowly, take everything as they went, having water and provisions with them. In this case it may be two days before the trouble is ended. It is presumed that the remains of Gen. Canby and Commissioner Thomas will be forwarded to this place, and they should arrive to-morrow some time.

Another carrier would leave the headquarters of the military camp this evening, and would arrive here early to-morrow. Those are all the particulars of the tragedy, in addition to the dispatch sent this afternoon. A courier left here at 9 o'clock to-night for General Gillem's headquarters, with dispatches from Schofield.

By many persons it is believed that the Modocs are utterly desperate; will fight till the last man falls, and that they will not leave the caves in the lava beds. By others it is believed that they have already made their escape, and will begin a relentless war upon all the weak parties of whites they encounter. It is supposed that Scar-faced Charley and Curly-head Doctor were with the Indians who attacked Colonel Mason's position and that this attack was a blind to attract the attention of General Gillem from the conference between Captain Jack and his men and the Peace Commissioners.

By this time the public are throughly familiar with the murder of Gen. Canby and the Rev. Dr. Thomas. Lieutenants Sherwood and Doyle were lured out of camp by a white flag to have a talk, and then fired on. General Canby and the Peace Commissioners were talking with Jack Schonschin and a few other braves. Suddenly Jack said, "All right," and shot General Canby dead. Mr. Meacham was shot in three places, but may recover. He thinks he shot Schonschin in the abdomen. Dr. Thomas was killed instantly. Both his and the body of General Canby were entirely stripped and mutilated.

The indignation throughout the country was tremendous, and the government determined upon a war of extermination. Troops were rushed on to the front, and the American eagle prepared to swoop down upon the medicine flag of Captain Jack, General Canby's place was filled by General Jeff. C. Davis, a soldier who served bravely through the war against his Southern namesake. The army of the United States was supplemented by the Warm Spring Indians.

The following particulars were received at a later date:

"The assassination of General Canby has created a most profound impression on the military, and his life will be fully avenged. The noble old gentleman was stripped stark naked by the treacherous murderers, and his necktie was the only portion of his clothing found. It is now known that the Indians intended a general massacre of all the "Tyees" or chiefs. They expected Colonel Mason to come out and talk with them on the other side, where they hung out a white flag, but the officer of the day, Lieutenant Sherwood, was the only victim to their treachery.

Lieutenant Sherwood is still in a dangerous condition but hopes are entertained for his recovery.

Our signal station is now of immense service, sending messages to and from camp to camp. The Indians were out yesterday in their fortifications, and one of them had a large white flag on a pole, which he was swinging to and fro in imitation of our signal officers.

The Snake and Pitt River Indians are still quiet, but are watching the course of the conflict with great inter-

It is now, stated that Generals Canby and Gillem and the Peace Commissioners had a talk about Riddle's warning, and came to the conclusion that it was only a ruse of Riddle's to delay the negotiations. They had not the utmost confidence in Riddle's veracity; but on this occasion it seems he was right in his supposition.

The Rev. Dr. Thomas was a Methodist Episcopal clergyman from the west, and Mr. Meacham was a Quaker. Neither of them had been brought into prominence before their appointment on the Modoc Commission.

General Canby married Miss Louisa Ames, of Baltimore; neice of Bishop Ames, of the Methodist Episcopal Church.

On the 22nd the following dispatch was sent from the Lava Beds.

"For the past two days there has been a kind of a truce, as we have had no Modocs to fight with. *They have gone—it is uncertain where;* but I feel confident that before long we shall hear of their whereabouts, if not their departure."

On the 24th this dispatch was sent :

"The Warm Spring Indians encamped last night near the lake, between us and Colonel Mason's command. *We have not seen an Indian to-night, although a sharp lookout had been kept, from the signal station.* "Donald McKay is of the opinion they have left, as, finding his party had taken up a position between them and water, they concluded another attack was meditated. The Warm Spring Indians are to hunt them up at night, *in order to try and find where they have located.* Two squaws captured by Colonel Miller's battery were brought into camp yesterday. They stated that two Yainox Modocs had deserted from the band. They were probably the two seen by Ticknor travelling west in the direction of the Ypinox reservation.

"The reinforcements from San Francisco of two batteries of the Fourth Artillery will be here in about five days.

"The Indians are supposed to still have about thirty fighting bucks. *Donald McKay is of the opinion that they have gone in an easterly direction towards Goose Lake.*"

Immediately on hearing of the massacre, the following dispatch was sent to Gen. Gillem by Gen. Schofield :

"Please inform me fully of the situation, so I may send more troops if necessary. If the Indians escape from the lava beds I may send troops to operate against them from another direction. Let me know fully what you wish. I suppose you have force enough to destroy the outlaws unless they succeed in eluding you. Nothing short of their prompt and sure destruction will satisfy the ends of justice or meet the expectations of the Government.

   (Signed)   . JOHN M. SCHOFIELD."

The remains of General Canby and Dr. Thomas lay in state at Yreka in the Masonic Hall all day, and were visited by nearly the whole population. Over a thousand persons viewed the remains. At twelve o'clock about 300 children of the public schools passed in procession by twos. The coffins were wrapped in the national colors and strewn with wreaths and flowers. The remains of General Canby were forwarded to Portland by the afternoon's stage in charge of the General's aid,

Captain R. H. Anderson, who was met at Rosebud on Wednesday evening by a special train for Portland.

The remains of Dr. Thomas left for Redding by private conveyance at two o'clock in the afternoon.

A dispatch under date of San Francisco, April 14, says: "A special messenger returned to Yreka to-night from the lava beds. There is nothing definite from the seat of war; there had been no fighting up to the time he left. Ammunition and supplies had been crowded forward with despatch. The surgeon had extracted four bullets from Mr. Meacham's wounds, and there is little hope of his recovery. There were various rumors as to when an attack will be made. Some say to-day and some to-morrow; the commanders waiting the arrival of the Warm Spring Indian scouts; who are to be used between the lines of General Gillem and Colonel Mason's commands, they, with cavalry, making a third line and all advancing together from the north, south, and east of the lake to the West. It is believed the battle will be a hard one, and that no quarter will be shown to the Modocs. The Pit River Indians remain quiet and peaceable, but if the Modocs escape there will be danger.

Every horse in Hot Springs, Surprise Valley, and Big Valley is down with the epizootic.

On April 26th, a reconnoitering party composed of Companies K and A, Fourth Artillery, and Company E, Twelfth Infantry, left camp at half past seven o'clock in the morning, in the direction of the stronghold of the Modocs.

They were commanded by Captain E. Thomas of the Fourth Artillery. A dozen Warm Spring Indians were expected to cooperate on Captain Thomas's left. The troops having formed a line of skirmishers advanced without molestation, until they arrived at the foot of the bluff south of the lava beds, having, meanwhile, signalled to the camp that no Indians were to be found. On reaching the bluff the Modocs opened a severe fire, causing the troops to seek such shelter as they could find in the crevices, chasms, &c. As usual, the foe was unseen. The first position soon became untenable, owing to the fact that the Indians were able to deliver both a cross-fire and an enfilading fire, the enemy enjoying every advantage of position and knowledge of the ground. They were also well armed.

In more than one instance a Modoc has been known to have two or more Spencer rifles, enabling him to keep up a rapid fire from his natural or artificial breastwork of rock. The surface of the ground in many places is torn up by volcanic actions, which form crevices, and these are adaptable to the purposes of either hiding or for points of defence. In several instances the soldiers, knowing nothing of the topography, have come unawares on such fissures, and before they could escape were confronted with a wily Indian, rifle leveled and finger on the trigger. Death, or at least a dangerous wound, is the result.

It was impossible to estimate the number of Modocs wounded. It was reported that the Warm Spring Indians took four scalps. This may be the whole or it may be only a portion of the killed, the Modocs being very careful to destroy as far as possible all traces of their casualties, carrying their wounded into caves and burning the dead bodies. The wounded are supposed to be hidden in caves, but few of them have been seen so far. Justice to the memory of the gallant dead compels the record of the following well authenticated facts; When Captain Thomas found himself and his men surrounded by his vindictive foe, true to his nature as a soldier, he sought to cheer the soldiers on to the bitter end and obtain if possible life for life, and to sell their lives dearly, saying: "Men, we are surrounded; we must fight and die like men and soldiers."

In his noble efforts to sustain the courage of his small command he was ably seconded by Lieutenant Howe and Lieutenant Wright.

After receiving a mortal wound he buried his gold watch and chain among the rocks and emptied his revolver among the enemies before dying.

If living he would also write in terms of well deserved praise of the conduct of Lieutenant Harris, who was similarly situated. Captain Thomas, with a portion of his Battery K, Fourth Artillery, set an example of bravery and determination to his men, uttering some such sentiments as those already quoted. Not that it required such expressions to stimulate the men to deeds of bravery, when every man would willingly have followed either officer wherever they chose to lead; yet it showed the mutual confidence existing between them. Since they were to fall, it is a pity it had not been when opposed to worthier foes. Yet it is a mournful consolation that each, Captain Thomas, Lieutenant Howe, and Lieutenant Wright, the sons of soldiers met a soldier's death in defence of the Government and laws of the country. Of the men killed or wounded it is perhaps sufficient to say they showed their bravery with their blood—the former with their lives, the latter in total or partial disability.

The victory of the Modocs was complete.

The news of this defeat created quite a sensation in army circles where the three young officers who were killed were well known.

Captain Thomas was a son of General Lorenzo Thomas, formerly Adjutant-General of the army.

Lieutenant Howe was the son of Major Marshal Howe, on the retired list, and a son-in-law of General Barry, the commandant at Fortress Monroe.

Lieutenant Harris is a nephew of the late Bishop McIlvaine.

Army officers attributed this disaster to the ineffi-ciency of the cavalry, which was dismounted because of the epizootic.

The two batteries of artillery and the one company of infantry that were ordered to advance into the Lava Beds with such fatal results, were intended as a recon-noitring party to find out whether the Modocs had really absconded. The suspicion that they had, and a too confident presumption that they would not fight in a body, may explain the disastrous blunder of exposing two companies of brave soldiers to be shot down like dogs by an unseen foe lying in ambush. It seems too apparent that the Indians practised successful feints upon General Gillem. They made him believe, or at least suspect, they had fled and scattered, and thereby disarmed his wariness and entrapped him into an am-buscade. We accordingly lost, in killed and wounded, more soldiers than the whole number of fighting Modocs. On their part there was no random firing.

They were all expert marksmen, and from the places of concealment every shot told. It seems a great pity that General Gillem did not wait for the arrival of his superior officer.

After this defeat of our troops, General Davis arrived and took command of the Modoc expedition.

Gen. Davis found the soldiers disheartened by the disasters of the campaign and had to resort to many devices to arouse their flagging enthusiasm and increase their efficiency.

He began his work with a will and earnestness that won for him the sympathy and friendship of the officers and privates, and inspired them with confidence. He studied the situation carefully, utilized the experience of his predecessors, gave the wearied soldiers time to recuperate from the fatigues and mental excitement incidental to their rough fights in the lava beds, sent out scouting parties, had his men disciplined in Indian dodges, and put his first grand movement in operation.

About this time, it was discovered that the Modocs had escaped from their stronghold by three routes, and finally encamped on Snow Mountain, twenty miles South of Sorass Lake.

Fights without any decided results were taking place occasionally, causing the loss and wounding of our troops.

One such battle was fought at Dry Lake, on May 10th, our loss was as follows:—

Killed—James D. Totler, corporal, Company B; Adolphus Fisher, private, Company B.

Wounded—Louis Dunbar, scalp wound in the head; Peter Griffin, flesh wound in the left hip; Jesse Reeves;

corporal, fracture of the left arm; which was subsequently amputated ; Patrick McGuire, fracture below the right knee—right leg amputated below the thigh; Samuel McGlew, flesh wound in the right arm, cutting an artery; George Brown, flesh wound in the left leg; all of Company B. Michel Maher, of Company C, flesh wound in the right hip. All the above-named belonged to the First Cavalry.

Wassamucka and Lebastor, Warm Spring Indians, were killed, and Yonowiton, another scout, had his right arm fractured.

But, notwithstanding those successes of the Modocs, it seemed that the peace men in the Modoc camp were dissatisfied, and preferred to trust to the good faith of the palefaces.

Accordingly, fifty-five members of Capt. Jack's band of Modocs surrendered to our army. Fifteen of these were warriors, and the rest were women and children.

Captain Jack then had twenty warriors left, and he resolved to fight to the end; being relieved of two obstacles, viz ; the women and children, and the peace party among the Modocs.

After a series of reverses befalling our soldiers operating in the lava fields, their bravery was crowned with success. Deserted and in despair, the Modoc chief surrendered, a prisoner of war, and, with five captured companions, upon trial by court martial, was righteously condemned to death.

CHAPTER IX.

THE LAST SCENE OF ALL.

THE last day on earth of the condemned savages was distinguished by a big talk, which lasted from 11 o'clock in the morning until 4 o'clock in the afternoon of October 2d, 1873. The death sentence had not been officially made known to the Indians, though they had been able to learn something of their impending fate through their squaws, who had been permitted to occasionally visit them. On that morning Gen. Wheaton, accompanied by Post Chaplain Heugemborg and several other officers and gentlemen, visited the Guard-house. The thirteen Indians confined there were released from their cells and conducted to the main room. Captain Jack, Schonchin and Boston Charley sat down on the edge of the bunks used by the soldiers when off guard. The other Modocs distributed themselves on the right and left of Captain Jack, squatting on the floor.

The Chaplain, a venerable gentleman, opened the talk. He stepped forward and took Captain Jack warmly by the hand, saluting each of the other Indians in like manner. He then told them of Christ's coming and how he died for God's red children as well as His white children, and the certainty of salvation by repenting and accepting Him. He told them that their refusal to accept Jesus would result in the Great Spirit sending them to a dreadful place. He had as much authority from the Great Father above to tell them this as General Wheaton had from the Great Father in Washington to tell them they should have to die. The Modocs knew that they had wicked hearts and that they had done many bad deeds; but however wicked they had been, they could be saved. Applegate reduced this to jargon, and Dave Hill interpreted the jargon into the Modoc language.

The Indians all listened attentively to every word that was uttered. Schonchin and Jack were the most attentive. The chief scratched his head very often, his blanket falling down about his waist. Boston Charley kept his red blanket closely about him, and, though wearing a

wasted look, seemed as if he had resolved to die game and
to say nothing. Black Jim, the tallest, most athletic, and
best looking Indian in the party, sat down against the
wall on a roll of blankets. He seemed to be somewhat
impatient at the proceedings, though not at all frightened.
Barncho, alias One-eyed Jim, who was chained to Sloluck,
sat with his head buried in his blanket. Sloluck, a young
Indian, was very restless, changing his position very fre-
quently—now lying down on his side, covering his face
with his arms, then standing up and looking nervously
around.

After the chaplain had finished his exhortation, all
but the six condemned Indians were returned to their
cells.

General Wheaton then requested the chaplain to inform
the Indians of the decision of the President. The chaplain
did so in a few feeling words. As Dave Hill translated
the terrible news, not a muscle of their faces moved. The
restlessness of their hands, however, showed that the blow
went home. They seemed to be striving hard to maintain
their composure. After some moments of silence, Captain
Jack's lips began to move. His voice was low and feeble,
and was at first barely audible. He spoke as follows:

"I have heard the sentence, and know what it is; but I
feel that I am more innocent than Bogus Charley, Hooka
Jim, Steamboat Frank, and Shacknasty Jim. These in-
stigated the crime of which I am accused. When I look
in my heart I see no crime. These young men started
these murders. It is hard to rid them of their savage
habits. I was always in favor of peace. Bogus Charley
was the first to propose the murder of General Canby and
the Peace Commissioners. The young men of the tribe
were with him. I said no; but they had the power, and
carried me with them. We came near having personal
difficulties, and my life was in danger. When Bogus
Charley proposed killing Canby, Boston Charley was the
first to sanction it. Bogus said, 'If you fail to help me, I
will do it myself.' I feel that while these four men are
free they have triumphed over me and the Government.
I should feel better satisfied if they were brought to trial.
Bogus was a traitor to both sides. He told lies to the
Modocs, and he lied to Canby. I should like to see him
brought in here. I know that Shacknasty killed Canby
and shot Meachem, and Boston killed Thomas. After the

massacre, Bogus told me he knew the blood was on his hands, and that I would not be held accountable. Bogus wanted to kill Canby and Gillem."

General Wheaton, through the interpreter, asked Captain Jack why they killed Canby and Thomas—what they expected to gain by such action.

Jack replied, "I wished for peace, but the young men said they were not ready for peace. They wanted war, but they did not give their reasons. I did not counsel the Hot Creeks to go and fight. When I surrendered I expected to be set free. I hoped to live on Klamath Lake with my people."

He then asked if he might entertain any hopes of living. On being told that the President's order would be carried out, he said the Great Chief in Washington was a long way off, and he thought he (Captain Jack) had been misrepresented. If the Great Chief at Washington would come to see him he might change his opinion.

He was then told that the Big Chief's children numbered millions, and that he was guided by good men who represented him.

Jack then continued: "I do not wish to talk a great deal, and only about those things near my heart. I would like to have the execution postponed until the matter was made more clear."

On being told that the President's decision was not given without a great deal of thought, Jack replied: "I know, judging by the delay, he was not hasty in the matter, but I think he should have heard what I had to say."

The interpreter informed Captain Jack that General Wheaton advised him not to think of a reprieve, but to pay attention to what the Chaplain said.

Jack said he knew what the Chaplain had said was good, and he should follow the advice, and if they permitted him to live he would be a better man. "I would like," he said, "to live to die a natural death."

General Wheaton then asked if any of the others had anything to say, when Sloluck said: "I want to talk. White men call me George. I have been confined in the guard-house through misrepresentations. My child died yesterday, and I could not go with the mourners. Nobody here can say they saw me at the massacre."

Black Jim then said: "I see a great many men present, but I have no talk to make as Captain Jack talks. I al-

ways tell the truth, and am well known among my people.
I was wounded in the first fight at Lost River, and was
very sick for many months. My heart tells me I am a
good and strong man, and able to take care of the Modocs.
If Jack and Schonchin are killed, I should then be left to
take care of the tribe. I don't know what Jack and
Schonchin think about it."

Jack muttered something and shook his head.

Black Jim continued: "That's my idea. If I have been
guilty of these crimes and the law of white chiefs decides that
I should die, I am willing to die and not afraid to die. I have
been a long time confined without having a chance to talk. I
am afraid of nothing, and when it's war I am always in the
front rank. I think we should have some time to make arrange-
ments for our spirits in the other world. I would like to hear
the spirit man talk."

General Wheaton explained that the Chaplain had come for
that purpose.

Boston Charley then took a quid out of his mouth and expressed a desire to tell his speech. He created a decided sensation. He said: "You all know me; during the war it seemed to me that I had two hearts—one Indian and the other white.
I am only a boy, and yet you all know what I have done. Although a boy, I feel like a man, and when I look on each side of
me I think of these other men as women. I do not fear death.
I think I am the only man in the room. I fought in the front
rank with Shacknasty, Steamboat, Bogus and Hooka. I am altogether a man and not half a woman. I killed General Canby,
assisted by Steamboat and Bogus. Bogus said to me, 'Do you
believe that those commissioners mean to try to make a peace?'
I said, 'I believe so.' He said, 'I don't; they want to lead us
into some trap.' I said, 'All right—I go with you.' I would
like to see all my people and bid them good-bye to-day. I
would like to go to the stockade to see them. I see that if I
were to criminate others it would not amount to anything. I
see it is too late. I know that other chief men were not at the
bottom of that affair, and they did not take so prominent a part
in the massacre as the younger men. I know but little, but
when I see anything with my eyes, I know it."

Boston was then asked why they killed Canby. He said that
all the presents they had received had no influence on them, and
they suspected Canby and the Commissioners of treachery, and
their hearts were wild. After the young men had decided to
kill the Commissioners, he told Bogus he was afraid. Bogus
said: "Don't be afraid; I can kill him." After that, Captain
Jack said he would go and prevent it. The object of Bogus
going in that night to camp was to remove any suspicion from

General Canby's mind. The young warriors thought that Canby, Thomas, Meacham and Gillem were powerful men, and that the death of these Tyees would end all further trouble. When they saw Dyar coming in place of Meacham; they decided to kill them all. When Bogus came into the soldiers' camp he told Riddle's squaw that he was going to kill Canby and the Commissioners. She said, 'All right; go and kill them.' I am telling what I know to be the truth—nothing more."

Captain Jack then referred to what Boston had said about his share in the massacre, and remarked: "Scar-faced Charley is my relative. He is a worse man than I am. I would propose to make an exchange, and turn Scar-face over in my place, and then I could live and take care of my family. I would like to make friends with General Wheaton and punish the right parties."

This modest proposition caused considerable amusement, much to the disgust of the chief. He concluded: "If I am to die, it is well. I am ready to go and see my Great Father above."

After a long pause, and none of the Indians manifesting any desire to speak, General Wheaton asked Schonchin if he wished to say anything.

A pleased expression stole over the old chief's face, as he assented and arose. He spoke for over an hour. His speech was the oration of the day, and made a marked impression.

Schonchin spoke as follows:

"You all here know me. I was always a good man. There never was a time that I did not want a white man's heart and asked advice from white men. I sent my boy to Yainox Reservation, and he chose a piece of land for his home. Boston Charley told the truth when he called me a woman. I was like a woman, and my voice was against war. I was always a peace man;" but there were some young men that were rash and anxious to distinguish themselves, Hooka Jim and some other boys made all the trouble, and when I look at the irons on my legs I feel that they should wear them. "I have always given the young men advice, shook hands with the whites, and here I am now, condemned, with irons on my feet. I heard what the Great Spirit man had to say, and I think it good. I should not die for what others have done, but I will not find fault with the decision, but will go to meet my father in the spirit land. My own father lived and died long ago when I was a boy. I often thought I should like to go and meet him in the brighter world, with the Great Spirit. If the law kills me and I go up to the spirit land, perhaps the Great Spirit will say to me, 'Schonchin, my law has taken your life, and I accept of you as one of my people.' It was not in my heart to do wrong, but

I was led away oy the wishes of the young men who were anxious for war. You know whether I am good or not, because you tried the law on me. Hooka Jim always thought he was a strong, good shot, and did these things contrary to my wish. I spoke against the murder of the Commissioners. When the big Chief in Washington read the evidence all over he must have been led to believe that Schonchin was a wicked, savage Indian, and did not know that Schonchin had used all his influence with the young men to keep them from doing these rash acts. The great Chief has to depend on the evidence he gets from his subordinates, and perhaps thinks Schonchin a bad, wicked man, while Schonchin has been a good, quiet Indian all the time. The Great Spirit, who looks from above, will see Schonchin in chains, but he knows that his heart is good and says: 'You die; you become one of my people.'

"I will now try to believe that the President is doing according to the will of the Great Spirit in condemning me to die. You may all look at me and see that I am firm and resolute. I am trying to think that it is just that I should die, and that the Great Spirit approves of it and says it is law. I am to die. I leave my son. I hope he will be allowed to remain in this country. I hope he will grow up like a good man. I want to turn him over to the old chief Schonchin at Yainox, who will make a good man of him. I have always looked on the younger men of our tribe as my especial charge, and have reasoned with them, and now I am to die as the result of their bad conduct. I leave four children and I wish them turned over to my brother at Yainox. It is doing a great wrong to take my life. I was an old man and took no active part. I would like to see those executed for whom I am wearing chains.

"In the boys who murdered the Commissioners I have an interest as though they were my own children. If the law does not kill them, they may grow and become good men.

"I look back to the history of the Modoc war, and I can see Odeneal at the bottom of all the trouble. He came down to Linkville with Ivan Applegate; sent Ivan to see and talk with Captain Jack, who talked no good. If Odeneal came by himself, all the Modocs would go to Yainox. I think that Odeneal is responsible for the murder of Canby, for the blood in the Lava Beds, and the chains on my feet. I have heard of reports that were sent to Yreka, Ashland and Jacksonville, that the Modocs were on the war-path, and such bad talk brought Major Jackson and the soldiers down.

"I do not want to say my sentence is not right; but after our retreat from Lost River I thought I would come in, surrender and be secure. I felt that these murders had been committed by the boys, and that I had been carried along with the current. If I had blood on my hands like Boston Charley, I could say, like him, 'I killed General Canby'—'I killed Thomas.' But I have nothing to say about the decision, and I would never ask it to be crossed. You are the law-giving parties. You say 'I must die.' I am satisfied, if the law is correct.

"I have made a straight speech. I should like to see the Big Chief face to face and talk with him, but he is a long distance off—like at the top of a high hill, with me at the bottom, and I cannot go to him; but he has made his decision—made his law, and I say let me die. I do not talk to cross the decision. My heart tells me I should not die—that you do me a great wrong in taking my life. War is a terrible thing. All must suffer—the best horses, the best cattle and the best men. I can now only say, let Schonchin die!"

The Chaplain now stepped forward and offered up an eloquent prayer. The venerable man wept like a child at its conclusion. The big talk then closed, General Wheaton telling the condemned that he would endeavor to comply with all their wishes. Afterward the squaws and children of the condemned men were taken into the guard-house to take a last farewell. The anguish of the women was frightful. The camp resounded with their hysterical groans.

On the morrow, October 3rd, the troops formed in line at 9 o'clock in the morning on the parade ground, under the direction of Adjutant Kingsbury. Captain H. C. Hasbrouck was in command of the line. The troops took position in the following order: Light Battery B, Fourth Artillery, Lieutenant S. W. Taylor; Company E, Twelfth Infantry, Lieutenant H. R. Anderson; Company F, Twenty-first Infantry, Lieutenant P. Jocelyn; Company G, Twelfth Infantry, Sergeant Ash; and Troop B, First Cavalry, Major Jackson. The Artillery acted as cavalry and, as well as the latter, were mounted. At 9.15 the column was placed in motion. On arriving opposite the Guard-house they halted. An interval was left in the centre of Company F (the central company). In this space a wagon drawn by four horses was place at 10 o'clock.

The morning was beautiful and clear. The gallows was located in an open field, to the south of the stockade, with a low undergrowth of brush to the east about forty feet. The procession moved to the gallows at 9 : 45 A. M. The drums were muffled; and the infantry marched with arms on the right shoulder, and the cavalry with sabres drawn. A great cloud of dust heralded their approach. Boston Charley and Black Jim sat in front of the wagon, and Captain Jack and Schonchin in the rear. Captain Jack kept his blanket drawn up nearly to his ears. Boston Charley leaned forward and intently surveyed the gallows. Nearly three hundred Klamath Indians, squaws and bucks, arrived at the fort at daylight, mounted on ponies. They dismounted and took up a position behind the troops. Boston Charley and Black Jim ascended the scaffold first. Boston Charley took a quid of tobacco as he stepped out of the wagon, and another as he walked up the scaffold stairway. He was very indifferent, looking around at the soldiers and spitting vigorously.

Captain Jack was very weak, and had to be helped into the wagon at the guard-house and assisted to his position by Corporal Ross. Boston wore Lieutenant Cranston's cap, and Black Jim a brown-felt slouch hat. Captain Jack and Schonchin were uncovered. Black Jim wore a full dress soldier's coat and blue pants ; Schonchin, an army blouse and blue trousers. Captain Jack wore a striped cotton shirt, which was open at the breast, revealing a red-flannel shirt. He wore trowsers of dark-mixed material. The Indians sat down on the scaffold, and were first pinioned, under direction of Colonel Hoge, by Corporal Thomas Ross of Company G, Twelfth Infantry ; Corporal John Killian, Battery B, Fourth Artillery ; private Eugene Anderson, Company F, Twelfth Infantry, and private Robert Wilton, Company G, Twelfth Infantry. At five minutes to ten, Applegate and Dave Hill mounted the gallows and explained to them that the orders that were about to be read were in relation to their sentence and execution. This occupied about five minutes. Schonchin, as Dave Hill descended the steps, turned round and spoke a few words to him.

Several wagons, filled with Oregonians, were corralled in the shade of some small pines to the right and front of the scaffold. After reading the orders relating to the execution, the Adjutant read the order commuting the sentence of Barncho and Sloluck. Four or five dogs belonging to the garrison basked in the shadow of the gallows, which was thrown forward—the bright sun being behind the condemned. Six coffins were stored under the gallows. At a quarter past ten o'clock Chaplain Heugemborg stepped forward and read the Episcopal service for the condemned prisoners. A gentle breeze swept across the field. After the Chaplain had concluded, Colonel Hoge, who had stepped down from the gallows, approached a bucket of water, lowered a dipper and took a drink. He ascended the gallows stairway, and directed a non-commissioned officer to carry some water to the condemned. Black Jim and Boston each swallowed a mouthful of water. Jack and Schonchin refused to drink. The nooses were then adjusted, the black cap was first drawn over Jack, then another placed on Schonchin, and another on Boston, Black Jim seeing the sunlight last. The caps consisted of black-canvas, condemned army haversacks. Three minutes of terrible suspense followed. The con-

demned were then compelled to stand up. Colonel Hoge took
out a white handkerchief and dropped it. At 10:15 o'clock,
precisely, Corporal Ross raised his hatchet, and with a flourish,
it severed the rope, and the drop fell with a report as though
one plank had fallen upon another. The four condemned fell
heavily. At the same moment, the clear voice of Captain Hasbrouck broke the awful stillness with the command, "In parade
—rest!" The four bodies swung round several times, and then
spun round the other way. Captain Jack never moved a muscle. Schonchin and Boston Charley died hard. Black Jim also
died without a struggle. The bodies were then cut down and
buried.

THE END

G# 17272180D